D0971327

NAILS, NOGGINS AND NEWELS

NAILS, NOGGINS
AND
NEWELS

An Alternative History of
Every House

BILL LAWS

SUTTON PUBLISHING

First published in 2006 by
Sutton Publishing Limited · Phoenix Mill
Thrupp · Stroud · Gloucestershire · GL5 2BU

British Library Cataloguing in Publication Data
A catalogue record for this book is available from the British Library.

ISBN 0-7509-3927-3

Typeset in 11/14pt Photina.
Typesetting and origination by
Sutton Publishing Limited.
Printed and bound in England by
J.H. Haynes & Co. Ltd, Sparkford.

Contents

Acknowledgements   vii
Introduction: Full House   1

1. OPEN HOUSE   9
Doors of Perception   9
Mr Chubb's Scandalous Lock   15
Mrs Coade's Dramatic Entrance   20
An Ingenious Idea: Jefferson's Automatic
    Door   21
Shaker Ann's Peg Rail   27
An Ingenious Idea: The *Therscwald*   28
An Ingenious Idea: The Perfect Porch   32

2. HOUSE STYLE   35
The Homely Proportions of Vitruvius   35
An Ingenious Idea: The Gothic Arch   38
Bungalow Taylor   40
The Adam Brothers' Complete Design   44
Willam Morris's Wallpaper   50
Mr Minton's Tile Revolution   57
An Ingenious Idea: Walton's Washable
    Wallpaper   58
Helen Allingham's Country Style   65

3. HOUSEHOLD ESSENTIALS   68
The Hand-Made Roman Tile   68
Joseph Aspdin's Cement   72
Thomas Whitty's Carpet   79

Count Rumford's Chimney   86
God's Best Boiler   91
An Ingenious Idea: House Tax   92
An Ingenious Idea: The Air
    Conditioner   100

4. HOUSE WORKS   103
Men of Glass   103
The Sliding Sash   111
A Question of Ascent   115
An Ingenious Idea: The Disposable
    Window   116
Mr Shanks's Flushing Loo   121
An Ingenious Idea: Gilbert Smith's
    Klargester   128
Mr Twyford's Bath   130
The Great Douche of Dr Wilson and
    Dr Gully   137

5. POWER HOUSE   143
William Armstrong's
    Hydroelectrically Powered House   143
The Candle-less House   149
Dame Haslett's Power Struggle   154
An Ingenious Idea: The Slot Meter   155
Leo Baekeland, Otto Bayer and
    Miracle Plastics   160
An Ingenious Idea: Underfloor Heating   162

Contents

The Sunshine Homes of George
Cadbury 170
An Ingenious Idea: The Photovoltaic
Cell 176

6. HOUSE PROUD 181
Flying Fitted Kitchens 181
Keeping Time 189
An Ingenious Idea: The Prefab 190

The True Aga Saga 195
An Ingenious Idea: Feng Shui 200
Home Do-It-Yourself 202
Franklin's Safety Rods 211
An Ingenious Idea: The Safe House 216
The Final Nail 217

Further Reading 221
Index 227

Acknowledgements

I could not have written this book if I had not served time as a somewhat inept builder's mate. Nor could I have produced it without the help of all those workers, former workers and enthusiasts who have tried to preserve their company histories.

I am particularly grateful to Richard Maggs and Dawn Roads of Aga-Rayburn; Richard Lawrence of Axminster Carpets; Beverley Longsden of Assa Abloy; Sam Rowlands at Avoncroft Museum of Buildings; Sharyn L. McCaulley of The Babcock and Wilson Company; Beatrix Zimmerman at Ein Unternehem der Bayer Business Services; Boulton Paul Heritage Project; the British Library; Alan Shrimpton and Diane Thornton at the Bournville Trust; Chedworth Roman Museum; David Birch at Celotex; Rebecca Chapman at Chubb Electronic Security UK; Simon Scott at Haddonstone; staff at Hereford College of Art library; Richard Forward and Anne Locker at the Institution of Electrical Engineers; Kim Curtis and staff at the Thomas Jefferson Foundation, Monticello; Mary Welsh and Michael Smith at KEE; John Garbutt of Kingspan Insulation; Marion Culley at Lafarge Cement; the National Trust; Julie Woodward at Pilkington plc; the Harry Ransom Centre; Les Smith at Royal Doulton; Sanderson; staff at the Society for the Protection of Ancient Buildings; Spillers of Chard; Rod Donaldson at Source; Terry Wooliscroft at Twyford Bathrooms; the Victoria and Albert Museum; Victoria Murray of VMPR; the Wolverhampton Archives; John Dowding at Wilton

Carpets; Jemma Roberts of Worcester Bosch and the Museum of Welsh Life, St Fagans.

Many others have contributed to these stories including Bobbie Blackwell, Hugh Bryant, Howard Hammersley, Graham Garner, Sandy Green, Peggy Laws, Tim Lambe, John Oxford, David Petts, Jerry Ross, Liz Rowse, Tom Schaefer, Richard Sidwell of Monmouth House Books, Dr Jill A. Warner and Annabel Watts. I am indebted to Jaqueline Mitchell and Hilary Walford for their editorial skills; to my agent, Chelsey Fox of Fox & Howard; and to my family, Abby, Sarah, Kahlia and Rosie, for their support.

All photographs are by the author unless credited otherwise.

Introduction

Full House

We live in an age of change, especially where our homes are concerned. Who calls at the hardware store nowadays to order stiles, rails and muntins, those essential components of the medieval door? Who fetches up at the do-it-yourself warehouse to fill their trolley with newels and noggins? (The newel was a constituent part of the staircase; noggins, derived from the Danish word *knog* meaning a wooden peg, initially referred to the bricks used to fill the framework in a half-timbered building, but then became common parlance for the blocks of wood used to reinforce partitions, roofs and ceilings.) Now we shop for flat-pack furniture, wood-grain, textured fibreglass doors, lumber from sustainable sources for our laminated floors and fitted kitchens (which are nothing of the sort). 'While new it is admired; when old, everybody will agree that it was always hideous,' suggests Charles L. Eastlake. He was writing in 1868.

With all the excitement over the hottest lifestyle ideas and the latest makeovers, it is easy to forget the intriguing histories that lie behind the four walls of the house. For every stick, stone and stitch in the fabric of the home was devised and built by someone, somewhere, once upon a time..

Country retreat: anything and everything in the home was invented by someone, somewhere, at some time.

Down the centuries this 'laborious class' has produced a virtual alphabet of inventions for the home, including air conditioning, baths, boilers, carpets, chimneys, concrete floors, doors, electric switches, fitted kitchens, gas lights, glazed windows, central heating, insulation, lightning rods, locks, nails, noggins, plastics, porches, sash windows, septic tanks, stairs, stoves, ceramic tiles, toilets, underfloor heating and wallpaper. 'From this fountain', noted William Hutton, 'do we draw our luxuries and our pleasures.'

Cross the threshold and your shadow falls on a multitude of long-forgotten inventions with a curious past: the peg rail that was a product of America's biggest religious cult; decorative tiles devised in the little Dutch town of Delft; a plastic light switch developed by an obsessive recluse destined to live – and die – on a diet of tinned food. Lock the door, draw the curtains on the windowed night and clamber into bed and you brush past a host of ingenious innovations, from a door lock devised by a blacksmith's apprentice (and scandalously picked in public by a New York lock maker) to an

Central heating was a distant concept when plans for this 1908 doctor's home 'with motor-house attached' were drawn up. The plans allowed for ten separate coal fireplaces.

expensive window-pane ritually broken when there was a death in the house. Stumble down the stairs in the morning and you encounter kitchen units developed by wartime aero engineers, a fireplace perfected by an American-born British spy, and a famous stove conceived by a blind Swedish Nobel Prize winner.

In *Nails, Noggins and Newels*, our first encounter with this history of the home is the front door, a place which has been constantly meddled with by the good and the great, including the world's most famous postman, Rowland Hill, and a man better known for his scientific theories on gravity than for his invention of the doggie door and the cat flap, Sir Isaac Newton.

Poised on the threshold and ready to turn the scandalised lock on the door, we glimpse the magical mystery doors at President Thomas Jefferson's home before encountering two women whose influence on the home still holds sway today. The first, Eleanor Coade, an astute businesswoman in the days before businesswomen legally existed, framed the doorway with elegant statuary and sculpture. The second, the equally remarkable Shaker Mother Ann Lee, inadvertently did so much to clear up the clutter in the hall.

3

Perfectly proportioned: the inner dimensions of the home were prescribed by a Roman engineer nearly two thousand years ago.

A tidy house is not necessarily a *stylish* house. House style is as important now as it was in 1903 when the pioneering American interior decorator Candace Wheeler was reminding her readers that the House Beautiful could 'dignify any circumstances, from the narrowest to the most opulent. We gather to ourselves what we personally enjoy,' she said, 'and will not take our domestic environment at second hand.' Yet we owe our home style to some very second-hand inventions: the proportions of our rooms, from the height of the skirting board to the position of the dado, were dictated by a Roman engineer around two thousand years ago. More mysteries surround the history of the staircase, not least because it is the second most haunted place in the house.

Meanwhile the concept of coordinated design, of matching everything from carpets to curtains and candlesticks, was dictated by two young men from Kirkcaldy around 200 years ago. These brothers brought the Adam style to Britain and the Federal style to America.

The question of what constitutes good and bad taste rests on shifting sands. 'The faculty of distinguishing good from bad design in the familiar objects of domestic life is a faculty which most educated people – and women especially – conceive that they possess,' declared Charles Eastlake, adding as an afterthought, 'how it has been acquired few would be able to explain.' Even as he committed his thoughts to paper in his *Hints on Household Taste* in 1868, two Victorians, William Morris and Herbert Minton, were

A home-grown stone house on the Outer Hebrides, its garden walls lined with old fishing floats. A campaign to 'electrify' even homes as remote as this was the work of former suffragette Caroline Haslett.

starting to transform the look of the average suburban villa. Their tasteful styles and designs endure to this day.

In 'Household Essentials' our innovators are more concerned with ingenuity than style, in roofing the house with Roman tiles, casting concrete floors, creating the forerunner of the fitted carpet, finding a solution to the smoking chimney and warming up, or cooling down, the home. These inventors provide the nuts and bolts of the home: Joseph Aspdin, the nineteenth-century Leeds bricklayer who helped to floor our houses with his Portland cement; the little Devon carpet maker who found a web of intrigue woven around his carpet loom; the British spy who Rumfordised our fireplaces, and the taxmen who profited by it; Mr Wilson, Mr Babcock and Mr Baxendale whose safety boilers were destined to become the biggest labour-saving device in the home (in the 1930s people spent an average of ten hours a week just keeping the home fires burning); and Willis Haviland Carrier who only developed his domestic air

Restoration nightmare in a cartoon of 1886: the invention of Portland cement has failed to ease the horrors of having the builders in.

conditioner when he noticed customers crowding around the commercial cooler he had installed in a department store.

In 'House Works' we turn to the functioning elements of the home and the men who made them. Pliny the Elder attributed the discovery of glass to a cooking accident on a Syrian beach, but it was 'the little master in the jacket', 14-year-old Robert Lucas Chance, who glazed the way for the more famous Mr Pilkington. Both men glazed the sash window, although the identity of its inventor remains a mystery: do we owe a debt of gratitude to a Dutchman, an American or a Yorkshireman?

Few today would choose to live without their bath, shower or, heaven forbid, the flushing toilet. The power shower was brought to its apotheosis by a brace of Malvern doctors, but it was more Victorian ingenuity, in particular the contributions of sanitation

Global design: the sliding sash window, seen here on a house in Toronto, has spread across the world. Was it invented by a Dutchman, an American or a Yorkshireman?

engineers like Shanks, Johns and Twyford, who put an end to the privy and the tin bath (not before, in America, Sangamon County's champion privy-builder demonstrated how the position of the privy could influence the height of the woodpile).

In the 'Power House', arms manufacturer William Armstrong lightened the darkness with his friend Joseph Swan's invention (despite his protestations to the contrary, Thomas Edison was *not* the father of the electric light); Pennsylvania's oil supplies helped to snuff out the candles; and a former suffragette opened the first all-electric home in Bristol to relieve the domestic drudgery of her sisters. Meanwhile the miracle materials invented by Leo Baekeland and Otto Bayer radically transformed the home, while an early trial with solar energy in the Birmingham suburb of a chocolate magnate turned to triumph.

Finally it's time to consider those elements of the home which are such a source of domestic satisfaction, from fitted kitchens, clocks and the true saga of the Aga stove to do-it-yourself and home safety, where Benjamin Franklin's rods and Feng Shui play a pivotal role. We go there safe in the knowledge that, despite the occasional DIY disaster, no home improver was ever sent to the gallows, at least according to Shirley Hibberd. William Hutton, meanwhile, uncovers the truth behind the half-naked women of Walsall – slave labour.

History can be unkind to inventors. Perillus of Athens invented a brazen bull for the execution of criminals (they were to be locked away in its belly and baked by fires lit beneath). He became the first man to die inside the bull. The medieval instrument of torture known as the Iron Cage was first tested out on its unfortunate inventor, the Bishop of Verdun. And Henry Winstanley, staying overnight in the lighthouse he had built on the Eddystone rocks off the Cornish coast, was swept to his death when a storm destroyed it in 1703. But is it a worse fate to be forgotten? The countless minor inventions that went into the making of our homes have been neglected for too long, along with the curious, the intriguing and the occasionally bizarre stories of the men and women who invented them.

1

Open House

Doors of Perception

Every culture in every corner of the globe has made the most of its front door. In eastern Europe farmers on Muhu Island off Estonia customarily decorated their doors with elaborate, geometric paintings, while southern Europe's Mudéjar craftsmen – Muslims working in Spain after the Christian reconquest – traced intricate patterns with nails in their metal-faced doors. In many countries a red door is auspicious, red being judged a lucky colour, although a red cross on a door in the Middle Ages marked a house visited by the plague. The front door was always a place for leaving signs, symbols and messages. The Revd Francis Kilvert, tramping through his Welsh borders parish to visit one of his flock, would leave a tell-tale on the door: 'At Rhos Goch Lane House no-one was at home so I stuck an ivy leaf into the latch hole', he wrote in March 1870. Spanish Arabs left their own welcoming message on the front door, furnishing it with door knockers shaped in the Hand of Fátima, the Islamic symbol of greeting extended to the stranger. In the west Christmas and Thanksgiving wreaths traditionally decorate the front door.

Inevitably people's taste in door furniture has sometimes verged on the vulgar. According to Charles Eastlake in his *Hints on Household Taste*

Estonian farmers made distinctive front doors, decorating them with elaborate designs which were also practical – the white paintwork made the door stand out in the dark.

The Spanish inherited a particular taste for decorated doors, such as this one in Valencia, from their Moorish craftsmen.

published in 1868 the most superior door knockers were to be sourced from Wurzburg in Bavaria. 'They . . . afford a pleasant contrast to the hackneyed portraits of tame lions and grinning satyrs which have been adopted as types of the modern door knocker.' But by 1908, according to Henry Walker, correspondent for *The Country Home*, the fate of the traditional door knocker was sealed by the invention of the electric bell. 'The knocker is doomed,' he lamented. 'The first nail in its coffin was driven when the wire bell-pull was invented, and it will receive its *coup de grâce* as the use of electric bell-pulls becomes more general.'

In his review of the door knocker Walker also reported on a bizarre feud over a precious door knocker at Brasenose College,

Oxford. It seems that in the fourteenth century resentment between students from the north and those from the south led to the northern students abandoning Oxford's hallowed towers and setting up their own hall of learning at Stamford in Lincolnshire. As if to remind themselves of old Oxford they took with them the door knocker from the door of Brasenose College, repelling an attempt by the Sheriff of Lincoln to retrieve it. While Oxford students were required subsequently to swear an oath 'not to attend lectures at Stamford', the aldermen of Stamford steadfastly refused to return the Brasenose knocker and the Oxford college had to perform a piece of subterfuge (by purchasing the Stamford building in 1888) to retrieve their missing knocker.

Meanwhile, the invention that Walker so feared, the electric bell, had been patented by Joseph Henry, the first director of the American Smithsonian Institute, in 1831. (It was a discovery that greatly assisted Alexander Graham Bell, who later remarked 'If it wasn't for his invention I'd never have invented the telephone.') Walker's fear that the electric bell would usurp the door knocker proved unfounded and the traditional panel and frame door, a design imported to England from Flanders in the fifteenth century, would have survived un-mutilated to this day but for the inventions of post-master Roland Hill and the dog-loving Sir Isaac Newton.

On 4 October 1892 George E. Becket registered a new invention at the US Patent Office. His device, he explained, was intended to be permanently secured to the door, 'having an opening or mouth formed therein increasing in width in a vertical direction from the front'. He called his invention a 'house-door letter-box'. Yet British carpenters had been cutting horizontal openings in their customers' doors since January 1840 when the former schoolmaster Rowland Hill launched his Uniform Penny Post. Many doubted that Hill's idea – charging customers to send mail with a pre-paid, gummed label – would ever catch on. A Penny Post had been introduced by London merchant William Dockwra in 1680, but by 1835 it would cost a

OLD MR. JONES AS HE APPEARED WHEN ASKED
FOR THE TWENTIETH TIME IF HE WOULD
HAVE HIS DOOR DONE.

'Mr Jones obstinately resisted the fashion for adding a new house-door letterbox to his home.' (*Punch*)

Humberside housemaid a day's wages to send a letter to her lover in Liverpool. The alternative was to send the letter 'caller collect', with the recipient paying on delivery. But it was said that unscrupulous senders simply wrote their message in secret code on the envelope. When the letter arrived the recipient read the code and then refused delivery, thus avoiding payment. Hill predicted that his Penny Post would prevent such frauds and persuade more people to use the postal system.

He was proved right. On the first day of the Penny Post the pre-paid mail trebled. Before long, plain Mr Hill had become Sir Rowland, his system of gummed labels (or 'stamps') was being copied across the world, and everyone wanted to deface their doors with a letter-box. As elegant Georgian doors, which had never seen a letter-plate, were subjected to a flurry of modernising carpentry work, ironmongers rushed out a range of ornate and decorative letter-plates, many of them, much to Henry Walker's relief, combined with a door knocker. In 1894 Henry Davis efficiently dealt with what might have become a new crime – stealing mail from the letter-box – with his 'improved Thief-proof letter-box'.

The invention of the cat flap and the dog door is attributed to the brilliant seventeenth-century mathematician who first formulated the law of gravity, Sir Isaac Newton, although the pet world had no serious impact on door architecture until the twentieth century. Until then the proper place for the dog was the doghouse outside, while the cat was expected to wait its turn at the back door just like anybody else. Gradually, as these animals wheedled their way into the warm kitchen, back doors began to be damaged and disfigured by spring-loaded, magnet-locking cat flaps and dog doors automatically controlled by passive infra-red eyes. One scientist even tried to patent a device that would trigger a nuclear strike on any neighbour's cat that tried to trespass on his own cat's door. The patent office regretfully refused his application.

This satirical cartoon of 1886 derides London's 'Knocker Boys', who, 'under peculiar *vinous* influences', had developed a habit of stealing door knockers. (*Punch*)

Mr Chubb's Scandalous Lock

Houselessness, the hero of Charles Dickens's *Uncommercial Traveller*, is trudging the London streets. 'Now and then in the night Houselessness becomes aware of a furtive head peering out of a doorway a few yards before him, and, coming up from the head, you find a man standing bolt upright to keep within the doorway's shadow, and evidently intent upon no particular service to society.' Pitted against those intent on breaking down the back door and performing 'no particular service to society' was a contraption that had made millionaires of its inventors, the Chubb family. 'Chubb locks were the first exhibits we regularly inspected and they really are wonderful, of every shape and size. He [John Chubb] explained to us the ingenious manner by which an attempt to force the lock is discovered,' wrote the effusive Queen Victoria in her diary for 10 June 1851 after meeting Mr Chubb at the Great Exhibition at Crystal Palace, London. She had reason to be grateful; her Tudor predecessor Henry VIII was obliged to take his portable Beddington lock with him and have it screwed to the bedroom door wherever he stayed.

As official lock makers to the Prince Consort, the Victorian Chubb family enjoyed prestige and power. No one, least of all John Chubb, was prepared for the scandal that would be unleashed when a young American picked Mr Chubb's most famous lock *in public*.

John's father Charles Chubb and his uncle Jeremiah had been brought up in the pastoral peace of the Hampshire village of Fordingbridge, where, as Henry Longfellow would have it,

> Under a spreading chestnut tree
> The village smithy stands.

It was to a Winchester smithy that both boys were apprenticed. In his early 30s Charles Chubb opened a naval ironmongery shop in Portsmouth. The year was 1804, the year before Admiral Nelson

Charles Chubb 1772 - 1846

Jeremiah Chubb came up with the design for a revolutionary house lock after his brother Charles opened his ironmonger's shop in Portsmouth in 1804.

routed the French fleet at a little-known place called Trafalgar. Business was brisk, and it became considerably brisker following a serious robbery in the Portsmouth dockyard when thieves opened a dockyard lock with a set of duplicate keys. The government offered a £100 reward, not for the return of the stolen goods but for a better lock – a lock that could be opened only with its own key. In 1818 Jeremiah designed the Chubb Detector Lock, won the government prize and patented the product.

Until then most householders had relied on an old-fashioned bar across the door to secure their homes, which was a fine arrangement as long as there was someone at home to lift the bar

16

Fig. 172.—Chubb's Original Detector Lock.

The Chubb Detector Lock resisted all attempts to pick it, including the efforts of an imprisoned locksmith.

on their return. An alternative was a primitive lock with a specially shaped plate, fixed over the bolt, which was supposed to prevent any but the correct key being slipped inside. The plate, however, was easily forced. For smaller items, such as a sea-chest or kitchen dresser for example, there were keyless locks, which relied on combinations of numbers or letters. These had been in use in England since the early 1600s:

A cap case for your linen, and your plate,
With a strange lock that opens with A.M.E.N.

run the lines of one early seventeenth-century play.

Mr Chubb's new lock was a revelation. To publicise it Chubb adopted the sales methods of his rival Joseph Bramah. Bramah had patented his own Bramah safety lock in 1784 and offered a reward to anyone who could pick it. Jeremiah similarly offered a £100 reward, and a convict and former lock maker languishing on one of the prison ships moored in Portsmouth's docks took up the challenge. The government doubled the odds by offering the felon a free pardon if he could pick the lock. But he could not and, resigning himself to his continued stay behind bars, he declared it the most secure lock he had ever handled.

The convict's testimonial spurred on sales, and between them the Chubb brothers sold over two and a half million Detectors in the next fifty years. They won a royal warrant for their products and in 1828 let it be known that even the Duke of Wellington had chosen to make his London home safe with a Chubb lock. Ironically it was Wellington's defeat of Napoleon at the Battle of Waterloo in 1815 which made the door lock so essential. The war left the continental markets depressed and some 400,000 redundant British soldiers roaming the countryside. Crime, and more significantly the fear of crime, soared.

Those of a nervous disposition could choose to move to the safest town in England, Willenhall in Staffordshire. Willenhall, with neighbouring Bilston and Wolverhampton, was the home of the locksmith industry. By the 1850s there were 340 small lock makers in the town, which was nicknamed Humpshire by mocking neighbours, a reference to the lock makers who, having spent their working lives bent over their benches, developed curved spines and hunched backs.

In 1851 the Chubb and Bramah locks were both put forward for the Great Exhibition, that showcase for all things inventive. Bramah was now offering £200 to anyone who could pick his lock. The looming 'Great Lock Controversy' would see both Bramah and Chubb pay up.

The man behind the scandal was the New York salesman and lock maker Alfred Charles Hobbs. He had visited the Exhibition and bought himself a fine lock made by Charles Aubin of Wolverhampton. Shortly afterwards he presented himself at Great George Street in Westminster, London, and announced his intention to pick the unpickable Chubb lock on display. He did so in just 25 minutes. Bramah's lock was his next target. It took a lot longer – 44 hours spread over sixteen days, but finally Hobbs publicly picked the lock.

The nation was horrified. Nervous widows trembled in their beds. Wealthy home-owners purchased large, dangerous guard dogs. One correspondent wrote a letter to *The Times* newspaper to reassure its readers, commenting that, 'our English locks . . . previous to the celebrated "lock controversy" of 1851, had borne a high character for skilful construction, beauty of workmanship, and undoubted security'. Lock manufacturers pointed out that no burglar would ever have the opportunity to spend 44 uninterrupted hours picking a lock. Such remarks reassured neither the public nor the bankers and insurance companies who, naturally, took the locksmith's craft seriously. The Royal Society of Arts was persuaded to mount a major public relations exercise and to offer a prize for the perfect, unpickable lock. A Mr Saxby, amid almost audible sighs of relief from the industry, duly collected the prize for his winning design. The resilient Mr Hobbs then stepped forward and picked the lock. In three minutes.

Only when a police superintendent declared in public that he had never known a burglar unpick a Chubb lock in his twenty-seven years' experience was public confidence restored. Hobbs's success led him to found his own locksmiths (taken over, ironically, by Chubb in the 1960s) while Mr Chubb, his pride somewhat dented, continued to lock the nation's doors for another century.

Having weathered the scandal of the picked lock, the Chubb business empire went into the production of house safes. (*Chubb Electronic Security UK*)

Mrs Coade's Dramatic Entrance

The attention lavished on an entrance way was always intended to indicate the level of craftsmanship inside. And creating a good impression in the eighteenth century was an all-consuming passion for those of a certain class. England then was a peaceful and prosperous place. The population was expanding and there was talk of building whole new terraces of smart town houses in Bath, London, Dublin, Cheltenham and Tunbridge Wells. The scene was set for a golden age for the house. The building boom stimulated demand for decorative stonework, for keystones, pillars and pinnacles, for caryatids and cherubs, for balusters, finials and front steps – anything, in fact, that drew attention to the house's

Jefferson's Automatic Door

The earliest door was no more than a curtain of animal skin, draped like a Mediterranean fly-screen across the entrance. The transformation from animal hide to panelled door came by way of many minor inventions, the most useful one being that of the eighteenth-century cast-iron butt hinge, still in use today. But the progress of door technology must surely have appeared to guests of Thomas Jefferson in the 1780s to have reached its apotheosis. Here at Monticello, his home in Virginia, stood an elegant pair of mahogany-framed, glass-partitioned doors, leading from the hall to the parlour. When one door opened, its twin opened too, as if by magic and with no visible

The rising butt hinge was a revolutionary invention that allowed the door to rise clear of the carpet.

mechanical means. Not until the 1950s, when the floors were removed during a major renovation, were the secret workings of the doors revealed. The door maker had hidden beneath the floor two drums, each fixed to a pivot at the base of the doors; when one door was opened, a chain wrapped around the drums gently and discreetly pulled open the second door.

It took over two years to have the doors made. Despite being, as Jefferson described him, 'skilled in the orders of architecture', the joiner James Oldham could not at first lay his hands on enough 'good lumber for the purpose'. Then he could source no kiln-dried timber. If Richmond builders 'do all their housejoinery with green stuff they are much behind even what I had expected,' grumbled Jefferson.

entrance. As the quarrymen and masons fell behind with their orders a remarkable woman, Eleanor Coade, arrived on the household scene, determined, despite her gender, to make a living from this explosion in home building.

'Mrs' Coade (the title was a Georgian courtesy: Eleanor Coade never married) took over a factory opposite the Houses of Parliament at King's Arms Stairs, Narrow Lane, Lambeth, to meet the insatiable demand for every kind of architectural ornament. Before long the factory was making gate piers, fountains and figurines, mermaids and sphinxes, Medici vases, nimble water nymphs and Bacchanalian processions, which could be set so they seemed to dance along the chimney-piece. The Coade catalogues listed sculpture that could be bought by the yard and, most important of all for those who wished to make a grand entrance, there were lions designed to stand guard on either side of the door and the heads of river gods intended to be set above it, sandwiched between rusticated voussoirs.

The business had been established by Daniel Pincot two years before, but he lacked Coade's Midas touch. He struggled (and ultimately failed) to survive the building trade's prejudice against its product, artificial stone. As he put it:

> The masons are decrying the material and deterring modellers from working in the manufactory; telling them they will be despised by the whole trade as forwarding a work which it is their interest to suppress . . . Again, when their employers signify an inclination to use this material, they immediately cry out 'Oh Sir! Why will you have artificial stone? It is but an imitation, a mere makeshift. Is it not more to your credit to have real stone than to stick up earthenware?'

The essential elements of Eleanor Coade's 'mere makeshift' (she described it as artificial stone) were rumoured to have been

Eleanor Coade marketed her doorway decorations, such as this river-god head in Bedford Square, London, across the world.

contained in a secret formula, which she took with her to the grave in 1821. But the base material, clay, was as common as the process to which it was submitted and from which it earned its name: *cotta* meaning baked, and *terra*, the Italian for earth.

Eleanor Coade may have used the term artificial stone rather than terracotta in order to prevent the Treasury slapping the same tax on it that they had on bricks, also a baked earth product, between 1784 and 1850. She marketed her artificial stone as the exotic-sounding Lithodipyra, from the Greek *litho* (stone), *di* (twice) and *pyra* (fire). The mixture of pre-fired clay, sand, flint and culet or crushed glass was set in a mould and then fired for up to four days at such a high temperature that it vitrified into a material with the texture of ceramic and the strength of stone.

Coade stone, as it became known, was 'calculated to answer every purpose of stone carving having a property peculiar to itself of resisting the frost and consequently of retaining that sharpness in which it excels every kind of stone sculpture and even equals marble itself,' reported the *Gentleman's Magazine*. The author was apparently unaware that Eleanor Coade's workers, far from carving the stone, merely cast it in specially made moulds.

Where Daniel Pincot had struggled, Coade triumphed. The timing of her marketing was especially astute. Recent discoveries of classical Roman pieces at Herculaneum and, in 1748, immaculately preserved in the volcanic ash of Pompeii, had whetted the aristocratic appetite for classical pedestals, Italianate chimney-pieces and neo-classical statuary. At the same time legislation was introduced to force Londoners to remove the ornate but dangerously combustible timberwork that decorated their town houses to reduce the risk of another Great Fire. This created a new market for fireproof porches, portals and steps.

Before long Eleanor Coade was working for some of the great architects and builders of her day, men (and they were all men) such as John Nash, the man who rebuilt London's West End and Buckingham Palace and the Adam brothers, Robert and James. Aside from public works such as the dignified lion that still stands on the south side of London's Westminster Bridge or the tomb of Captain Bligh (of the *Bounty*) in the Lambeth churchyard of St Mary, Mrs Coade's stone was used (and is still to be seen) decorating doorways in Bedford Square, the only complete Georgian square remaining in London, and at the home of the architect Sir John Soane at Lincoln's Inn Fields in Holborn (now the John Soane Museum). Soane, who designed the Bank of England, was an important architect in London in the early 1800s and he designed his own home to reflect the fashionable trends of the time with two Coade stone figures over the entrance. The Royal Academy painter J.E. Hodgson failed to see the attraction: 'Its façade is singularly mean, to which meanness a touch of vulgarity has been added by two plaster figures perched upon the cornice,' he wrote.

24

Once condemned as 'mere makeshift', Coadestone, being frostproof and fire resistant, outlived its critics and influenced the twenty-first-century fashion for stylish entrances.

When she opened a gallery on Westminster Bridge Road in 1798, Coade transformed the entrance way with an elaborate 'Stone Sculpture' which she also copied on to her trade card. 'The anatomical parts of these statues are worthy of observation,' she promised. (A set still supports a porch at Schomberg House in Pall Mall, London.)

Coade stone was exported across the world. In Rio de Janeiro the gates of the city zoo were cast in Coade stone to replicate the Brentford gateway at Syon House, designed by Robert Adam. However, a commission for two chimney-pieces for The Octagon, an eighteenth-century house in Washington, now owned by the American Institute of Architects Foundation, called into question her good name when the fireplaces arrived without the mantelpiece. 'Mr [*sic*] Coade ought to be Mr Shark', complained the owner, Colonel Tayloe. The later dispatch of the missing sections – and a number of royal appointments from both George III and George IV – restored her reputation and ensured that Eleanor Coade did not, as her father had, die in penury.

In 1784, when she was 51 years old, Eleanor Coade could afford to give her new home, Belmont in Lyme Regis, Dorset, a full, Coade stone facelift. Belmont, later the home of writer John Fowles, had been owned by her uncle and was known as Bunter's Castle. In November 1821 Eleanor Coade, 'sole inventor and proprietor of an art which deserves considerable notice', reported the *Gentleman's Magazine*, died at Camberwell aged 89. A religious West Country woman, she had established a successful business in the days when wives were forbidden by law to control their own affairs. When she died she left her wealth not only to the poor of the parish of Lyme Regis, but also to three married women with strict instructions that their husbands should not lay a finger on their wives' bequests.

The Coade stone empire continued under the direction of William Croggan, a distant cousin whom Eleanor had appointed to manage the business when she was in her 80s. Although he had lucrative contracts for Coade stone work for Buckingham Palace, Croggan was bankrupted in the 1830s by a notorious debtor, the Duke of

York, who failed to pay his bill of £20,000. In 1838 Eleanor Coade's original factory moulds were sold, many of them to the former employee Mark Henry Blanchard, whose own artificial stone work would figure prominently in the Great Exhibition of 1851.

Architectural bodies have continued to argue over the use of artificial stone ever since, even while specialist conservators were being commissioned to repair some of Mrs Coade's originals. She, meanwhile, would have been gratified to find that her invention had percolated down through society and can now be found in the form of false urns, figurines and fountains enhancing the entrances of urban homes everywhere.

Shaker Ann's Peg Rail

The hall is a crowded thoroughfare. Crossing the threshold into the hall we enter the place for air-kissing dinner guests, manoeuvering pushchairs and falling over the dog. It's also the resting place for overcoats, raincoats and waterproofs, and, although the rail from which these items hang rarely earns a second glance, the provenance of the peg rail is a curious one. Brought to a state of creative perfection by a remarkable Mancunian woman and her religious visions, the peg rail was a faultless piece of Shaker design and one which profoundly influenced modern Scandinavian style.

The trail of the peg rail begins in Toad Lane, Manchester, home of the young, independent-minded Ann Lee. It was the 1700s. The established Church was under attack from dissenters and Ann Lee had already earned a reputation for disrupting church services. She joined a Quaker group run by Jane and James Wardley at Bolton-le-Moors, a village just north of Manchester. The Wardleys had come under the influence of a group of French religious refugees, the Camisards, who brought their own brand of mysticism to the English shires in the early 1700s. By the time Ann joined them the group had been nicknamed

The *Therscwald*

Newly wed wives and New Year's Day first-footers are still welcomed across the threshold in superstitious re-creations of pagan customs that promise to bring good luck and fertility to the family. In ancient times people believed that the necessary rituals had to protect the first person to cross a new threshold. It may well be that some of our contemporary, civic ceremonies, formally laying the foundation stone or burying a time capsule beneath a threshold, for example, hark back to these ancient rites.

But why the threshold? Why should our doorways be considered a suitable place for threshing – that is, thrashing the corn to separate the wheat from the chaff?

In the not so far off days when the harvest was still a hand-made affair, threshing was a traditional domestic task carried out on every farm and smallholding. The words of the folk song, and the fate that befell poor John Barleycorn, describe the process:

> Then came men with great sharp scythes
> To cut him off at the knee
> They bashed his head against a stone
> And they used him barbarously
> Well then came men with great long flails
> To cut him skin from bone
> The miller has used him worse than that
> He ground him between two stones.

In dry southern climes threshing could be done in the open, but in northern climes the farmer needed a dry, sheltered place with storage space on either side, the first for the sheaves of corn, the second for the threshed straw and the bagged-up grain. A barn, open at the front and back to create a natural wind tunnel where the chaff was blown aside, was the perfect solution. But before the barn became available, the farmer used his own house, built with the front door directly in line with the back door in order to create the necessary through draught. And the place where the corn was threshed with a crab-tree stick, a flail or the Anglo-Saxon threshing bar (the *wald*) was the *therxold* or *therscwald* or, as we still call it today, the threshold.

The threshold, where grain was threshed. The wind, whistling through the house, helped separate the wheat from the chaff.

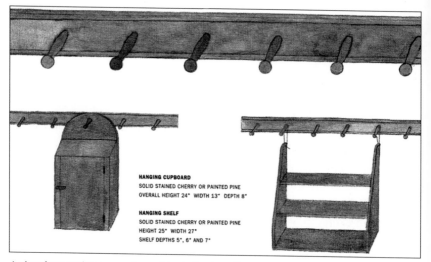

HANGING CUPBOARD
SOLID STAINED CHERRY OR PAINTED PINE
OVERALL HEIGHT 24" WIDTH 13" DEPTH 8"

HANGING SHELF
SOLID STAINED CHERRY OR PAINTED PINE
HEIGHT 25" WIDTH 27"
SHELF DEPTHS 5", 6" AND 7"

A place for everything . . . and everything in its place. The peg rail is one of the Shakers' most useful legacies. (*Illustration Tim Lambe*)

the Shaking Quakers, a reference to Jane Wardley's habit of delivering her religious revelations with a shake and a tremble.

Ann married one Abraham Standerin and bore him four children, but sadly not one of them survived. She was devastated by their deaths and fell into what clinical psychologists would diagnose as acute depression, but which Ann described as a means of cleansing herself from 'human depravity'. She became celibate, staying awake at night and pacing the room in her stockinged feet. When she stopped eating and drinking she became so weak that it was only her friends' intervention that saved her from death. As they nursed her back to health she started a campaign against the sins of the flesh:

> This blessed fire began,
> And like a flame in stubble,
> From house to house it ran.
> (*Millennial Praises*, 1813)

Mother Ann, as she became known, led night-long meetings with her fellow Shakers, sharing with them her visions for the future. In 1772 her voices told her that there was a place for them in America. Two years later she and a small group of disciples abandoned the grim streets of Manchester for New York and the new world.

The Shakers stayed in the city until they could raise enough money to buy a patch of wilderness called Niskayuna in Western New York State. Then they moved out, set up home and founded what would become the largest sect America has ever seen. Despite (or because of) their conviction that sex was the root of all sin and that to truly serve God one must remain unmarried and celibate, they managed to recruit 4,000 members and run eighteen communities. In the course of their history more than 20,000 Americans counted themselves as Shakers.

The Shakers were advocates of common property ownership and sexual equality. They lived communally in families of up to 100 members occupying large houses in New England, Kentucky, Ohio and Indiana. And here they did as Ann had bid: 'Provide places for your things, so that you may know where to find them, at any time, by day or by night; and learn to be neat and clean, prudent and saving, and see that nothing is lost.' Most items were stored in the vast cupboards that were a particular feature of the dwelling house – the cupboard in the Church Family House in Enfield, New Hampshire, contained no fewer than 860 drawers. But the devotees' cloaks, small cupboards, sweeping brushes – one was allocated to each room – and even shelves were hung from a special peg rail.

Made from local hardwoods – maple and cherry were favourites, but hickory served just as well – the rail had a modest beaded decoration along one edge. Rather than using conventional cow-hoof gum to fix the pegs to the rail, each peg was tapered to wedge it tight, or threaded so that it could be screwed into the rail. Pegs were set closer together where they were intended to carry cloaks or brooms, and further apart to hold the Shaker chair, made so that 'an angel might come and sit on

The Perfect Porch

The porch is an eminently practical device for keeping the rain out of your shopping bag while you fumble for your house keys. In its humblest form the porch manifests itself as the porch hood, a timber and tile or wrought iron and plate glass hat that sits over the door. The Bretons like them so much they use them to protect not only their front doors, but their cemetery gravestones too. A grander version of the porch is the *porte-cochère*, a roofed area large enough to shelter a carriage and protect the passengers from the elements as they walk to the door. 'It rains. And you are very surprised not to be wet on getting out of the carriage,' explained the 6th Duke of Devonshire in a letter to his sister about the new porch at Chatsworth House. 'That is owing to the new porch, built in wood, looking like stone; and to be built in stone some day or other, having been hastily put up for the Queen's visit in December 1843.' The modern incarnation of the *porte-cochère*, the Perspex-covered car-port or breezeway tacked on to the side of a house, serves the same purpose but it is a poor cousin in aesthetic terms.

The portico, an elegant entrance crowned by a low pitched roof and a pediment supported on columns at either side, is the ultimate expression of the porch. From the classic eighteenth century to the mock-classic twentieth century, the portico represents a graceful addition to the home – even if it fails to fulfil the original function of the porch, which is to keep you or your guests dry.

Making an entrance: a perfectly proportioned porch.

Top left: Folk style: the eaves of a cottage porch in Ireland, decorated with geometric designs. *Top right*: Sentrybox style: a sensible solution to the wet westerlies of the west coast. *Above, left*: Georgian style: a pillared portico, influenced by classical architectural ideas. *Above, right*: Victorian style: decorative bargeboards and turned columns reflect the florid tastes of the late nineteenth century.

it'. The angels were slightly inconvenienced since the chairs were hung upside down on the rail to prevent dust settling upon the seats.

Initially the peg rail was built into the house wall and the plasterwork carried up to the rail leaving only the pommelled pegs exposed. Beauty, insisted Ann Lee, rests on utility: 'Whatever is fashioned let it be plain and simple and for the good.' Just as Shaker gardeners would not raise flowers in their plots because they were too showy, the craftsmen (the 'aristocrats' as the field workers called them) avoided adornment. Another Shaker adage was 'Where there is no law there can be no transgression', and the carpenters defied traditional joinery practice by incorporating a curious little adjustable leg into the base of items such as candle sconces or shelves. When the peg rail was fixed to the wall rather than built into it, the leg would rest on the rail and keep the sconce or shelf upright.

Mother Ann died in 1784 and in the mid-1800s the Shakers, always happy to sell on surplus goods, went one step further: they set up a factory and started marketing their furniture in showrooms and through mail-order catalogues. In 1927 a Shaker rocking chair caught the attention of Danish architect Kaare Klint, an influential figure in the Scandinavian modern movement. When the Danish Co-operative Wholesale Society began to make well-designed and affordable furniture, it was the Shaker style that inspired many of its designers. By the 1950s, when the Finnish architect Alvar Aalto was producing his experimental steam-shaped birchwood furniture, the new Scandinavian style was flooding into European and American homes. Now no hall was quite complete without one of Mother Ann's famous peg rails.

In their 1997 catalogue IKEA offered a £19 'PS shelf with 5 knobs. Solid birch and lacquered fibreboard with steel knobs. Design: Tony Almén/Peter Gest'. There was no mention of Mother Lee. Meanwhile a small group of surviving Shakers living at Sabbathday Lake in Maine wait to see whether Mother Ann's prophecy will be fulfilled: she predicted that the movement would enjoy a second renewal once the numbers dropped to five.

2

House Style

The Homely Proportions of Vitruvius

Spare a thought for Marcus Vitruvius Pollio as you paint your skirting-board, fix a dado rail or tease out a paper roll to replicate a frieze beneath the ceiling. The man responsible for the presence and positioning of these domestic features died at least two thousand years ago, never dreaming that one day hordes of home decorators would be following his good advice.

While Vitruvius had some sense of posterity – he once declared that a person's prestige depended not on the work he did, but on its social relevance – we know less about the man than we do about his work. He is thought to have been an architect and the engineer responsible for looking after Rome's aqueducts. Some time between 23 and 27 BCE he sat down to write, or more probably dictate, his *De Architectura Libri Decem* or Ten Books of Architecture. In this work Vitruvius aired his views on medicine, mathematics and grammar, and published his famous life-study of a naked man spreadeagled inside a square and a circle – a figure later depicted by Leonardo da Vinci as 'Homo Vitruvianus'. He praised his creative colleagues: Ctebisius of Alexandria and Archimedes for their inventions, Aristossenes (Aristotle's apprentice) for his music,

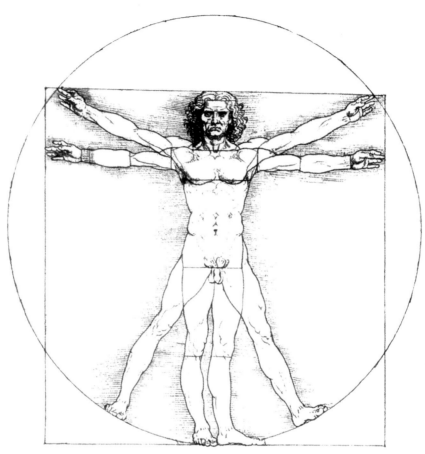

Leonardo da Vinci's *Homo Vitruvius*. Marcus Vitruvius's architectural writings celebrated the human form. They also dictated the presence of familiar items such as skirting-boards and picture rails.

Agatarch for his theatre and Terentius Varro for his architecture. But most important of all, Vitruvius detailed the building methods, materials, units of measure, correct proportions and styles of the buildings of ancient Rome.

Architectural symmetry and proportion were sacrosanct, he declared, as he proceeded to provide the exact proportions of the classic Roman building, the 'orders with capitals and entablature'. (In doing so he condemned future students of architecture to hours of study as they struggled to master the names, or entablature, of the classical column: architrave, astragal, cornice, corona, cyma recta, cyma reversa, dentil, fascia, frieze, fillet, modillion and triglyph.) The proper height of a room, he explained, was determined by the column itself, the correct height being ten times the diameter of the column. The thinner the column, the lower the room. Even where the columns were absent from the room, their ghostly presence would be

The classical orders, as advocated by Vitruvius, even made their mark on this timber façade at Tallinn in the former Soviet Union.

dictated by lines on the wall – which would become the skirting-board, dado rail and ceiling frieze or picture rail.

When the Italian architect Andrea Palladio first read Vitruvius he was overwhelmed: 'I ever was of the opinion that the ancient Romans did far exceed all that have come after them, as in many other things so particularly in Building, I proposed to myself *Vitruvius* both as my Master and my Guide, he being the only Author that remains extant on this subject,' declared Palladio. The fact that he could read and study Vitruvius's 'orders with capitals and entablature' was something of a miracle in itself. Although Vitruvius probably died peacefully around the time of the birth of Christ, his fate is unknown. The manuscripts of his *De Architectura*

The Gothic Arch

The best way to bridge the opening over a window is with a beam of wood. The lintel, from the French *limite* meaning to limit, has served as a sensible solution for centuries. The alternative is to place a temporary frame across the opening and build an arch across it. When the frame is removed the arch supports itself. Church builders in the Middle Ages customised the technique, creating stylised arches which turned 'not upon semi-Circles, according to the Roman manner . . . but meet in acute Angles, in Imitation of the Gothic Way of Building', according to the Tudor chronicler John Stow. Renaissance critics found the style uncouth, uncivilised and 'Gothic', a reference to the barbarous Goths who had sacked Rome in AD 410. However, by 1827 the Gothic arch had become 'the most beautiful and varied style of decoration', according to Nathaniel Whittock (in *The Decorative Painters' and Glaziers' Guide*), as Britain and America were smitten with Gothic Revival fever.

The window arch was an elegant and traditional solution to supporting the masonry above.

What had started as a fashionable sideshow with the Gothic redecoration of Horace Walpole's Twickenham home, Strawberry Hill, in 1753 had turned into a flood of Gothification by the early 1800s. Jerry-builders put up 'Gothick Villas' in the Castle Gothic style, characterised by battlements and crenellations, or Monastic Gothic with 'crockets and vaulting'. In America a flourishing Carpenter's Gothic produced a rash of stained-glass lancet windows, soaring bell towers, gargoyles, grottoes and decorative gables.

This torrent of Gothification did not meet with everyone's approval, however. J.C. Loudon complained about an epidemic of fake Gothic, 'generally, a very different thing from the correct Gothic designs supplied by architects who have imbued their minds with this style of art'. One of those 'especially imbued' was the architect Augustus Pugin, who declared the Gothic arch to be 'truly Christian' and the purest form of architecture.

The Gothic arch reached its apotheosis in the work of architects such as George Gilbert Scott, whose rood screen for Hereford Cathedral (now in the Victoria & Albert Museum) took the style to new heights.

Libri Decem, however, survived, thanks to the work of the Palace Scriptorium at the court of Charlemagne, the most powerful ruler in early medieval Europe. In the early 800s the Scriptorium operated like a sort of medieval photocopier, tracing and recopying classical manuscripts, including Vitruvius's *De Architectura Libri Decem*.

When in 1414 an Italian named Bracciolini discovered the Scriptorium's copy of Vitruvius's work, he thought he had stumbled on the complete architectural source book of the age. *De Architectura Libri Decem* was, his colleagues decided, the 'wisdom of the ancients'. It should be venerated and followed faithfully. It took another century for Vitruvius's work to be translated into Italian, but by then most of that country's architects were already devotedly following his lead.

Although the Roman elements of architecture would be challenged (notably by the English architect Inigo Jones and his French counterpart Salomon De Caus), Vitruvius's architectural contemplations were destined to dictate the appearance not only of most grand houses, from the Winter Palace of St Petersburg to the White House in Washington, but most of our everyday homes as well. Without Vitruvius there would be no skirting-board, dado or frieze. He may not realise it, but when the do-it-yourself decorator paints a stripe on the wall to fake a dado rail, or stencils a border to mimic a picture rail, he does so with the hand of Vitruvius firmly upon his shoulder.

Bungalow Taylor

The house with no staircase is the most popular domestic building in the world. Every nation has its own version, from the Hebridean *tigh dubh* (black house), the granite and thatched *pallozas* of Galicia and the mud-walled *rondevalles* of southern Africa, to the cob and thatched Devon longhouse or the Estonian *häärber*, a long, turf-

A vernacular version of the bungalow, the single-storey whitewashed *tigh dubh* (or black house) hunkered down on the Hebridean landscape.

roofed, log-walled cabin where the master's family lived at one end and the servants at the other.

The prototype for the modern bungalow was the cool Bengal *bangala*. 'Even Englishmen live in what are really stationary tents which have run aground on low brick platforms,' explained a district official in India in 1801. 'They are "bungalows", a word I know not how to render unless by a cottage.' Some were even air conditioned. Raised in an Indian Army bungalow at Peshawar, Peggy Leech recalled fan-shaped shutters under the eaves. 'A boy would be employed to sit on the verandah operating a fan inside the house by a string tied to the fan and passed through the fanlight to his foot.' Improvements on the basic design were not always a success: 'The flat roofs were thatched, but the thatch sheltered

Little tin palaces, created from cast iron, timber and tin-cladding, were shipped across the world.

snakes which had an irritating habit of crawling under it into your room. The thatch was replaced with corrugated iron, but that was very cold in winter and unbearably hot in summer.'

The design of these practical, Raj-style bungalows, duplicated in prefabricated sections by the building trade, was carried across the world, into the tea estates of Ceylon and the rubber plantations of Malaya, the depths of Kenya and the sheep stations of the Australian outback.

One of its earliest manifestations in northern Europe was built by a London architect, John Taylor, at Westgate on Sea near Margate in Kent in the early 1880s for Harley Street physician Sir Erasmus

A neat *bach*, set in a park at Rotorua in New Zealand, exemplifies the world's most popular house design.

Wilson. The design was judged such a success that Taylor teamed up with an Arts and Crafts architect, John Seddon, to build a seaside estate of bungalows near Birchington in Kent. They were expensive, prefabricated homes, each equipped with servants' quarters and wine cellars and, flying in the face of being completely stairless, a look-out tower. Taylor and Seddon's homes were marketed at around £10,000. (To put the price in perspective, a bungalow designed and built fifty years later by Edwin Stephens with 'bedrooms so planned that they are approached from the kitchen without the maid having to cross the hall' cost just £1300.)

Taylor and Seddon's bungalow estate attracted an artistic community including George Frampton (creator of the Peter Pan statue in Kensington Gardens, London) and the artists Solomon J. Solomon and Dante Gabriel Rossetti. (Rossetti died there and gained the dubious honour of becoming the only member of the romantic Pre-Raphaelite movement to pass away in a bungalow.) The houses also boosted sales of a new book of plans published in 1891, *Bungalows and Country Residences* by Robert Alexander Briggs, nicknamed Bungalow Briggs for his troubles. Briggs's plans contributed to a rash of bungalow building in Britain, so much so that the Society for the Preservation of Rural England was formed in the 1920s to halt this single-storey invasion. It singularly failed to do so. Now, from the Australian lodge house and the New Zealand *bach* to a piece of Dallas-style real estate in California, the bungalow reigns supreme.

The Adam Brothers' Complete Design

The Oval Office at the White House is perhaps the best-known room in the world, and yet it owes its elliptical origins to two of America's least-known brothers. In America the style came to be known as the Federal style. In Kirkcaldy, Scotland, where the brothers came from, it was better known as the Adam style. For some observers its qualities were obscure. 'What is now universally known as the Adam style has become so familiar that many people recognise it immediately, almost instinctively, though perhaps without knowing exactly why,' declared one commentator, Michael Wilson.

Despite being two centuries old, the Adam style still makes its mark on contemporary homes: a semi-circular fanlight over a front door or glass panels set on either side, oval shaped rooms and vestibules, fine plasterwork decorated with plaster swags and urns – all are typical Adam features. The Adam brothers, however, went further. They were fastidious in their makeovers, coordinating the colour schemes for the rooms they designed and ensuring that everything from fireplace to fingerplates matched up. When they published their *Works in Architecture* in 1773, they laid claim to a

44

new decorative style, 'a revolution in the whole system of this useful and elegant art'. It was true. They had anticipated the role of the interior designer by two hundred years.

Their style was a conscious reaction to Palladianism, a style of architecture and interior decoration inspired by the Italian architect Andrea Palladio. The Palladian style, itself inspired by the classical styles of ancient Rome, had revolutionised town and country houses in Britain and North America in the eighteenth century. Now, in the final forty years of the 1700s, Palladianism was running out of creative steam. Worse still, its very pedigree was being called into question by certain heretical ideas, namely that classical architecture was based not on the works of Vitruvius and the Romans but on those of the earlier Greeks. Many establishment figures simply refused to countenance the idea, and the Italians were naturally scandalised. It was left to the enquiring Dilettanti Society, founded in 1732, to send observers into the field, to Italy, Greece and the Adriatic, to seek out the truth and pen the evidence in their sketchbooks. When they returned to publish their findings, the awful truth dawned: classical architecture had originated in Greece, not Rome.

The revelations caused a schism in architectural circles with one side declaring itself for Rome and the Romans and the other for Greece and the Etruscans. Some simply kept their own counsel and watched to see which way the wind of fashion was blowing – and it proved to be blowing towards two men who borrowed freely from both sides and opposed any rigid ideas on classical architecture: Robert and James Adam. Their father, William Adam, was one of Scotland's leading architects and his four sons, John, Robert, James and William, all followed him into the trade. John stayed in Scotland, while Robert and James set up in England in 1758 and William concerned himself with the financial side of the English business (somewhat unsuccessfully, for he died in poverty in 1822).

Robert, born in 1728, embarked on the almost obligatory Italian tour before setting up the family firm in London together with

James, William and two of their sisters. The company was never short of work. Their interiors, much more than their exteriors, elicited much comment and inspired much imitation. Robert and James insisted on total design, planning everything from the shape of the room – they liked to create circular, octagonal and oval rooms and rooms with apsidal ends or alcoves – down to the colour of the carpet and the style of the curtains. Their plasterwork was a particular trademark, the traditional heavy, florid plasterwork of the previous age being replaced with what they called 'a beautiful variety of light mouldings, gracefully formed, delicately enriched, and arranged with propriety and skill'.

Those skills lay in the hands of a team of artists and craftspeople, including two plasterers both, confusingly, named Joseph Rose (more confusingly still, both baptised their sons Jonathon), and a portrait painter, Angelica Kauffman. Kauffman, who painted panels for the Adam brothers, led an extraordinary life. She was born in Switzerland in 1741, and her father, himself a painter, fostered her artistic talents. By the age of 12 she was painting a commissioned portrait of the Bishop of Como; by 25 she had settled in England and, under the patronage of Sir Joshua Reynolds, was helping to found the Royal Academy. After a disastrous marriage to a swindler, 'Count' Frederick de Horn, she obtained a legal separation and married the artist Antonio Zucchi, another member of the Adam team.

Another Adam craftsman was the soon-to-be-famous potter Josiah Wedgwood, who was producing a range of plaques and panels in his characteristic blue and white jasperware for the brothers. Wedgwood was to profit from one of Robert Adam's white lies. When a client queried the origins of the design of some vases, Adam explained that they were copies of original Etruscan pottery. The fiction of the fashionable vase gained sufficient credibility for Wedgwood to market 'Etruscan' pottery, which he manufactured at his new pottery works in Burslem. Astutely he called the place Etruria.

The Adam brothers produced design features such as this ceiling decoration, probably painted by Angelica Kauffmann in the 1770s.

The Adam style was not welcomed by everyone in the backbiting social circles of the eighteenth century. One architect, an Adam rival, called it puerile ornament. Horace Walpole dismissed it as 'gingerbread and snippets of embroidery'. He described entering one room, which was heavily decorated with Mr Wedgwood's artefacts, as 'like going out of a palace into a potter's field'. Even the voluble Dr Johnson had his reservations. Visiting one of the Adam masterpieces, Kedleston Hall in Derbyshire, he found the pillars there 'too very large and massy . . . they were better away'. King George III's own architect, Sir William Chambers, said to be a dour and humourless individual, described the Adams' work as mere decoration and 'filigrane toy-work'.

Nevertheless the Adam style had popular appeal. Formulated during the reign of King George III, the monarch who famously 'lost' America, the style crossed the Atlantic along with an emigrating army of plasterers, joiners, carpenters and metalworkers in the late 1700s. Following on from the Georgian Colonial style, the Adam style introduced features such as plaster garlands and windows symmetrically arranged around a central front door or flanking each side. The craftspeople knew how to execute the new style and the increasingly wealthy Americans were more than happy to pay for it.

But what should this pioneering style be called? Georgian Colonial had become a household name in America: the Adam brothers had not. To describe the style as Georgian, or more properly late Georgian, would have seen America's most successful colonial house style named after the monarch who had waged war on its people. Thomas Jefferson (whose Monticello mansion was firmly rooted in the alternative, classical style) had only recently completed his draft of the Declaration of Independence, which signalled the final split with Britain and the odious King George. Tactfully the new style was termed Federal instead.

The fashion for all things Adam started to founder in the 1800s when a more casual approach to furnishing a room was adopted. In the late 1700s furniture did not fill the room but rather, lined its walls, partly because the assembled company needed to circulate, and partly because of the vogue for vast skirts. As a consequence, while fine Adam chairs might be richly ornamented at the front, they were as plain as brown paper at the back. The ability of furniture designers and cabinet makers like Thomas Chippendale to replicate and improve on the Adams' popular designs – and, unlike the Adam brothers, to provide them with an attractive backside – did the family business no good. Nor did a series of ill-fated speculative developments by the Adam family in London. In the end the American War of Independence brought down the Adam empire. It had cost too many prospective British customers too much cash and they could no longer afford to pay for the authentic Adam makeover.

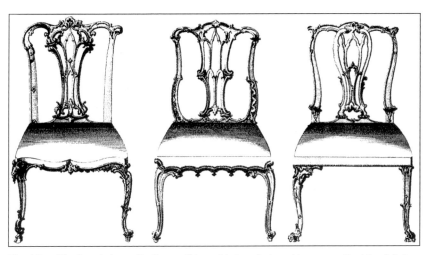

The ability of furniture designers like Thomas Chippendale to replicate and improve on the Adams' designs stole a march on the brothers. (Thomas Chippendale, *The Gentleman and Cabinet-Maker's Director, 1762*)

But the Adams' all-in approach to interior design had made its mark. A century later it was resurrected in America by the textile designer Candace Wheeler. She founded the New York Society of Decorative Art to further the work of women and their handicrafts and to promote the idea, perfectly acceptable now, slightly outrageous in the 1880s, that women had a sharp eye for good interior design. 'A woman feels that the test of her capacity is that her house shall not only be comfortable and attractive, but that it shall be arranged according to the laws of harmony and beauty,' she wrote in her *Principles of Home Decoration with Practical Examples*, published in 1903. Convinced that women could do the job without the interference of men, in 1883 Wheeler set up Associated Artists, a women-led company which celebrated the Arts and Crafts style and which became one of the first and most successful interior decoration firms in the country.

The difficulty in the early twentieth century was that most women were still shackled to their husband's income and career. The woman, wrote Wheeler, is expected 'to train her children according to the latest . . . enlightened theories', involve herself in 'philanthropic movements' and express a political opinion. 'These are things which are expected of every woman who makes a part of society.' And, she pointed out, 'no less is it expected that her house shall be an appropriate and beautiful setting for her personality, a credit to her husband, and an unconscious education for her children'. The multi-tasking woman proved perfectly capable of taking it all on board – unlike the Adam brothers, who only had to cope with the whims of their clients.

William Morris's Wallpaper

Oscar Wilde, a dramatist to the last, is reported to have declared on his deathbed at the Hotel d'Alsace, Paris, in 1900: 'My wallpaper is killing me; one of us must go.'

It was difficult to be enthusiastic about wallpaper a century earlier. While the French-invented *papiers de tapisserie* were a popular enough substitute for pricey tapestries, wood panelling or leather-covered walls, they were still expensive. But things were about to change. A machine invented by the Frenchman Louis Robert, and designed to produce a single, continuous roll of paper, was about to go into production in England. Early experiments at mechanically printing wallpaper – the first machines were powered by horses – had been modestly successful, but from the 1840s the technology improved rapidly. Within thirty years machines capable of accurately printing twenty-four colours on a single sheet were clattering out acres of wallpaper. Affordable wallpaper was now available to anyone with a rented villa and a decorator's calling card.

Most decorating firms still produced hand-printed papers, which were generally regarded as superior to machine print except by those who made them: men and women regularly worked a fifteen-hour day on the mechanical printing presses, but it was preferable to the slow poisoning suffered by the hand printers, from the lead and arsenic in the pigments. Mass production in the UK, and later America, put these two nations ahead of their European rivals in terms of volume, but both flagged behind when it came to original patterns and designs. James Shirley Hibberd insisted: 'The Home of Taste is a tasteful home, wherein everything is a reflection of refined thoughts and chaste desires,' adding that, in such a home, 'vulgarity, meanness and vice dare not cross the threshold'. Nevertheless, the average bank clerk or grocery store owner who chose to paper over the cracks with home, rather than foreign, wallpapers was faced with a series of novel, but dull, designs. 'If the French beat us in art, we now have the palm for cheapness,' remarked a correspondent, dryly, in the *Journal of Design* in 1849.

Charles Locke Eastlake was not impressed: 'When did people first adopt the monstrous notion that the "Last pattern out" must be the best?' he demanded to know in his *Hints on Household Taste* in 1868. 'Is good taste so rapidly progressive that every mug which leaves the potter's hands surpasses in shape the last which is moulded?' He remonstrated that commonplace taste 'lined our walls with silly representations of vegetable life, or with a mass of uninteresting diaper'.

Augustus Pugin, who spent the last years of his short life working on the Houses of Parliament and who designed more than a hundred wallpaper patterns for that building, once acidly remarked that British wallpaper patterns were 'a great favourite of hotel and tavern-keepers'. The British government of the day endeavoured to improve matters by setting up state-funded design schools, while an influential group of artists and designers led by civil servant Henry Cole established the Design Reform group and a publication, the *Journal of Design*, to try to staunch the flow of dull, flowery patterns. It was to no avail. Production rates rose (the *Furniture Gazette* of 1879 reported that Americans were buying annually enough wallpaper to paper round the world) but so did the rush of garish and ghastly designs.

One man and one movement not only reversed the trend, but gained lasting popularity, proving to be still a worldwide best-seller in the late twentieth century. The man was William Morris, and his Arts and Crafts movement transformed the world of wallpaper and interior design. By the late 1800s the few designs such as Daisy (1864) and Jasmine (1872) that he dashed off between weaving, writing and striving to hold together a failing marriage were on sale across the world. When the *Titanic* sank in the Atlantic in 1912, it went down with a full complement of William Morris wallpapered state rooms.

Morris was born on 24 March 1834 in what was then the country village of Walthamstow on the edge of London. His parents were wealthy and his father, also William, was an enthusiastic medievalist who regularly took his young son on trips around England's churches and cathedrals. Long before he left home to study beneath the limestone spires of Oxford, Morris had gained a good understanding of (and a romantic longing for) the craftsmanship of the Middle Ages.

At Oxford Morris proved to be a gifted, if not a very diligent, student. He discovered a kindred spirit in his new-found friend Edward Burne-Jones: both abhorred the materialistic, machine-driven society of the day and both looked back on the pre-industrial age with nostalgia. The time would come, they agreed, when the inspired artist would work in harmony with the honest, labouring craftsperson. The idea of a combined arts and crafts movement was about to be born.

Morris travelled abroad looking at the medieval tapestries of Northern France and Belgium, then returned to Oxford to join an architectural practice. He stayed with the firm just long enough to

William Morris, who advised: 'Have nothing in your house that you do not know to be useful and believe to be beautiful,' (*Sanderson*)

William Morris's designs, such as Corncockle, were influenced by the natural forms he found in his garden at the Red House. (*Sanderson*)

befriend a fellow student, Philip Webb, who was later commissioned to design Morris's Red House, before he left for London and the bohemian life. Sharing lodgings with Burne-Jones, Morris became involved with the Pre-Raphaelite artists Dante Gabriel Rossetti, John Everett Millais and William Holman Hunt. He explored every conceivable field of the arts and crafts, experimenting with stone-

and wood-carving, with ironwork and glass, with fabric and paper. 'Everything made by man's hand has a form, which must be either beautiful or ugly,' he announced in one of his later lectures: 'beautiful if it accords with nature, and helps her; ugly if it is discordant with Nature, and thwarts her.'

The practical experience of working on the Red House gave Morris the confidence to found the firm of Morris, Marshall & Faulkner, 'Fine Art Workmen in Painting, Carving, Furniture and the Metals', in 1861. He liked to tell his friends how he lived over the shop as he instructed them to 'have nothing in your houses that you do not know to be useful and believe to be beautiful'. He turned his hand to wallpaper designs, adopting flower-strewn backgrounds, as in Daisy, based on an illustration from a fifteenth-century manuscript, and Jasmine. Morris had filled a series of sketchbooks during the fertile Red House period and his stylised wallpaper patterns with their images of sunflowers, pomegranates, roses and acanthus leaves drew heavily on the Red House days.

The new middle classes, meanwhile, were thirsting for inspiration and ready to buy into the whole Morris experience. While Morris & Co. offered a bespoke service to prestigious customers, it also catered for this mass market. Although Morris and Burne-Jones espoused the craft of hand-printing, the business of rolling out enough wallpaper to meet the expanding demand required the services of another company, Jeffrey & Co., which machine-printed mile upon mile of Morris's designs. Curiously Morris himself had no fondness for the wallpapered finish: although his first design, Trellis, a latticework entwined with dog roses and decorated with blue birds, papered his daughter May's London bedroom, the artist preferred to decorate his walls with tapestries or paintings by his friends.

Morris died in 1896, and a painted farm wagon wreathed with willow and bullrushes carried his plain oak coffin into Kelmscott churchyard in the Cotswolds for burial. By this time his wallpaper was on sale everywhere from Boston to Berlin and from New York to

Morris preferred to decorate his own walls not with wallpaper but with tapestries that he designed and wove himself.

Melbourne. In 1904 Hermann Muthesius, an attaché at the German Embassy in London, wrote a comprehensive review of English interiors, *Das Englische Haus*. He noted: 'Some of Morris's papers are as popular with the public today as they were forty-five years ago.' William Morris, he declared, was the 'father of modern wallpaper'.

Over the next sixty years various eminent artists, Walter Crane, Niki de Saint-Phalle and Andy Warhol among them, designed patterns for wallpaper, but reproduction Morris wallpapers continued to sell. Even postwar America, now taking a Modernist lead in interior design (eclipsing European supremacy for the first time) continued to buy Morris wallpaper to complement their homely colonial style.

In 1940 Morris's original designs were bought by Arthur Sanderson, a firm that had been importing luxury French wallpapers in the days when William and Jane Morris were building the Red House. Twenty years later Crown, which provided wallpaper for more than half the homes in Britain, introduced several new designs that would have shocked a dog. They were meant to. 'This is a young wallpaper. It isn't going to please everybody. Your old Aunt Emily will probably hate it. She also hates mini-skirts, fast cars and Pop. We aren't trying to please Aunt Emily,' declared Crown. The design did not outlive Aunt Emily. Sanderson, meanwhile, avoiding the shock of the new, started to hand-print the Morris designs using the original wooden blocks. They sold well. A century after he had sketched out his first designs, William Morris was back in favour.

Mr Minton's Tile Revolution

Quarry tiles, paviours, ceramic tiles, decorative mosaics, unglazed porcelain tiles – it's hard to imagine a world without tiles. But tiles are a product of peace; in times of war tile development slows and production dwindles. In times of prosperity this slab of baked earth reaches new heights of excellence and ingenuity, just as it did in the Dutch town of Delft in the 1700s.

The craft of tile making had travelled slowly to Delft from the Turkish palaces of Sultan Suleiman, where vibrant-coloured blue, green and red tiles, manufactured at Iznik and Kutahya, decorated the inside and outside of the buildings. The tile makers, passing on the secret of their metallic glazes from one generation to the next, carried the craft across North Africa and into Spain. From southern Spain the master makers of the lustrous arabesque *azulejos*, the glazed ceramic tile, took their tile works to the outskirts of Valencia,

Walton's Washable Wallpaper

In 1836, according to J.C. Loudon, every section of society was using wallpaper: 'Walls and ceilings of "Plain Cottages" are seldom panelled on account of expence [sic] other than by painted lines or coloured paper,' he reported. Elsewhere the parlour walls of the average Victorian villa required no less than three wallpaper treatments – up to the dado rail, the filling above and finally the frieze. Regular replacement was expensive but necessary. The standard, non-washable distemper paints used on wallpapers were quickly spoiled by smoky oil lamps, dusty house fires and sticky hands. What everyone wanted was a hygienic 'sanitary' paper that did not harbour germs and was washable.

In 1864 Frederick Walton set up a factory at Staines in Middlesex to make a new hessian-backed carpet from linseed oil, resins and wood pulp which he called linoleum. In 1882 he had covered patterned wallpaper with a mixture of oxidised oil and cork. He called this, the first washable wallpaper, Lyncrusta Walton. Walton had originally intended his hardwearing paper to mimic leather wall coverings, but its 'sanitary' nature appealed not only to the Victorian villa owner but also to civic authorities, who adopted it for their town hall walls. Lyncrusta continued to protect walls with its armour-plate-like finish for a century. In 1887 Thomas J. Palmer, the former showroom manager at Walton's London store, patented a cheaper version of washable wallpaper, made from cotton fibre pulp. He borrowed from the Greek to describe it as Anaglypta, meaning a raised-up engraving, and successfully exhibited it at the Manchester Royal Jubilee Exhibition in 1887. It was an immediate hit and both Lyncrusta and Anaglypta were to continue on sale, virtually unchanged, for the following century.

to the now run-down districts of Manises and Paterna. Here they refined their methods, decorating the traditional tin-glazed tiles with freehand paintings executed in bright, new pigments – lemon yellow and magenta, emerald green and Seville orange. The ceramics were shipped out through Majorca to Italy, where the Italians called the pottery *maiolica* after Majorca. When the majolica tile makers of Faenza in Italy took the same techniques to France, the pottery was dubbed *faience*.

Religious dissension, meanwhile, was driving Protestant families out of Catholic-dominated southern Europe and they, with the tile makers among them, moved north to the Low Countries and into towns like Delft. Delft was not the only commercial centre for tile making, but it was fast becoming one of its most important producers with tile painters there concentrating on their trademark blue and white 'delftware'.

'Father had been a tile maker, his fingers still stained blue from painting cupids, maids, soldiers, ships, children, fish, flowers, animals on to white tiles, glazing them, firing them, selling them,' reports Griet, the heroine in Tracy Chevalier's *Girl with a Pearl Earring*. The year is 1664 and Griet must go and earn her keep since her father, blinded by a kiln explosion, can no longer work. As she leaves to clean the studio of the portrait painter Johannes Vermeer, Griet takes a gift from her father. It is a Delft tile, painted by him, of a boy and a girl walking along together.

The designs were not original. The Protestant tile owners, past masters at copying, had duplicated the fashionable blue and white Chinese porcelain imported by the Dutch East India Company – which had an office in Delft – during the early 1600s. When in the 1650s civil war in China shut the trade routes to that country, the townspeople of Delft cornered the market.

The white glazed decorated tile, as practical as it was pretty, was used around the home in the low-lying Netherlands. Majolica or faience tiles were too light to tile the floors, but they made a useful

Griet, the girl with the pearl earring, a victim of the Dutch tile trade. (*Girl with a Pearl Earring*, by Peggy Leech after Johannes Vermeer)

and waterproof wall covering. Being fireproof and easy to clean, they also made a functional surround for the fireplace. Within a few years of Vermeer's supposed indiscretion with young Griet, Dutch tile makers had travelled across the English Channel and established themselves in the port cities of Bristol, Liverpool, Glasgow and London. Each city developed its own decorative tile style, from Bristol's white on white (*bianco-sopra-bianco*) to Liverpool's polychromatic designs.

Dutch delftware survived and thrives still. But fashion is fickle. By the start of the nineteenth century the British delftware tile makers had run out of business. Yet within fifty years of their collapse a new generation of tile makers was struggling to keep pace with an insatiable demand for floor and wall tiles. Today there is scarcely a house or apartment that does not have a tiled surface somewhere. What happened to make the household tile so irresistible? Enter Herbert Minton, the master tile maker who would help tile everyone's walls and floors too.

In 1793 Herbert Minton's father, Thomas, had set up a factory producing porcelain, bone china and cream-coloured and blue-printed earthenware majolica in Stoke-on-Trent. With its natural reserves of coal, clay and cheap labour the Staffordshire town, already busy with pottery works, was an obvious choice for Minton. Mintonware sold well, especially when Thomas Minton added his new blue willow pattern to the range of bone china dinnerware. In 1835, the year before his father's death, Herbert Minton brought out a novel catalogue of floor tile styles based on medieval patterns of encaustic tiles. It was a clever marketing move. The Victorian passion for archaeology, in particular for excavating medieval sites, had helped revive the hard-wearing encaustic floor tile. Encaustic tile making was once a flourishing monastic industry, but the kilns turned cold after the dissolution of the monasteries, and the techniques were largely forgotten until excited antiquarians began rediscovering medieval tiled floors such as the one at Byland Abbey in North Yorkshire.

Herbert Minton turned around the centuries-old craft of tile making and made the household tile into the must-have material of the twentieth century.

Encaustic tiles, from the Greek *egkaustikos*, meaning to burn in, were made by pressing together a pattern of coloured clays, usually red and white, and covering the surface with a glaze before firing. Samuel Wright, a ceramicist and inventor, had patented his own method of encaustic tile making which involved pressing clay into a mould with a raised pattern set in the bottom. Once it had been fired for the first time the indentations in the pressed clay were filled with slip (a different coloured, liquid clay) and fired for a second time. The finished tile was smooth, strong and as strikingly attractive as any made by medieval monks four centuries earlier.

Herbert Minton bought up a share in Wright's patent. After a marketing breakthrough in 1843, when his chief engineer attended a soirée graced by, among others, the Marquis of Northampton, Prince Albert and the Prime Minister Sir Robert Peel, the Minton order books for encaustic tiles began to resemble the itinerary of some twentieth-century heritage tour, with Windsor Castle and Queen Victoria's retreat, Osborne House, at the top of the list. Minton's friend Augustus Pugin also did much to further the cause of the floor tile through his high-profile work at Westminster. (Only 37 when he died, Pugin was a gifted architect who designed not only the mock-medieval carving and panelling for the new Houses of Parliament at Westminster in 1835 but also most of the finer details, right down to the inkwells and hat stands. He was said to have paid more attention to the manufacture of encaustic floor tiles than to anything else.)

Minton, meanwhile, did not ignore the mass market for wall tiles. When in 1840 Richard Prosser patented his process for making clay buttons with clay dust, Minton recognised its potential for the mass manufacture of ceramic wall tiles. He bought a share in the patent and started turning out tiles at his Stoke factory. The introduction of a steam-driven press to replace the hand-turned tile press in the 1870s enabled the process to meet the growing demand for wall tiles as the British population doubled from twenty million to forty million in the second half of the century.

The tiles were the plastics of their day. 'To what use can tiles not be put?' asked a contributor to the *Pottery and Glass Trades Review* in 1878. 'Cornices and chair-mouldings, doorframes and windows are set with them; hearths outlined or made wholly from them, doors inlaid, and staircases decorated . . . summerhouses are gay with them, for the tile is always fresh and cool-looking in its bright designs, while nothing is warmer for winter rooms than the dark earth-coloured ones.'

Fishmongers and butchers easily dealt with the splash of cod gut and the smear of ox blood in their freshly tiled premises and persuaded their wives to decorate their own kitchens with transfer-printed tiles. Shopkeepers decorated their high street premises with wall-high, hand-painted tiled tableaux and ordered pretty, hand-painted tiled landscapes to decorate their front porches at home. Housemaids buffed a shine on their mistresses' majolica-tiled dados and tripped across cheap, plain quarry tiles in the kitchen. Entrance halls, corridors, conservatories, patios and even the garden pavements were floored with red, buff and brown encaustic tiles, occasionally with an added border in the more expensive blue and white tiles. The tile was carried through from cradle to grave: transfer-printed tiles with scenes from Aesop's fables lined the cheeks

Tile designs on the 1908 Michelin Building in Fulham Road, London, celebrated the race-winning tyres of the day.

of the nursery fireplace, and transfer-printed tiles with the image of the deceased were set in commemorative stones in the graveyard.

Minton was not the only tile manufacturer. 'The ware produced by Messers Maw & Co. of Salop stands almost unrivalled,' insisted Charles Eastlake in 1868, but even after Herbert Minton's death in 1858, and the succession of his equally dynamic nephew Colin Minton Campbell to the company, Minton remained a household name. In 1870 Minton's established an art pottery studio in Kensington, London, under the direction of the painter W.S. Coleman, to encourage amateur and professional artists to decorate tiles for the company. As well as Pugin, other notable designers and artists contributed to the tile maker's art, including Kate Greenaway,

C.F.A. Voysey and Walter Crane. William Morris reverted to the traditional blue and white colours of delftware for his own tile designs, while the creative painter William De Morgan adopted the great Islamic palette of blues and greens. The painter Winslow Homer and the architect Stanford White helped form the New York Tile Club, dedicated to furthering the art of the hand-decorated tile, while Arts and Crafts furniture makers incorporated tiles into their furniture. In the 1920s the Arts and Crafts designer C.R. Ashbee returned to the original Turkish factory at Kutahya to commission Islamic tiles for one of his projects.

Now no bathroom is complete without its tiled shower, no kitchen without its tiled splashback and no atrium without its tiled floor. As the author of 'How To Tile Your Walls', an article slipped into the 1950s *Home Management Guide* between 'Successful Home Dyeing' and 'How to Make a Gay Ovencloth', promised: 'Tiling, the ideal treatment for all larder, bathroom and kitchen walls, will last almost indefinitely.' Putting up tiles, promised the writer, was 'straightforward for the handyman' and even for the 'inexperienced housewife'. The household tile had come a long way since little Griet left home with her father's delftware tile tucked into her pocket.

Helen Allingham's Country Style

The first public housing initiative in Britain was launched in the 1880s to replace with modern homes not some crowded inner-city slum but thousands of folk-style, roadside cottages in the Irish countryside. The rural rebuild was a response to the 1861 census which revealed that three-quarters of the population was forced to live in single-roomed, mud-walled cottages. (One Sligo civil servant reported how a sick farmer, his wife and five children shared a home the size of a modern garage with the poultry, three cows, two calves, two pigs and a horse.) As the mud-walled Irish cabins were coming down, the cottage homes of south-east England were suffering a similar fate, but this time at the hands of home improvers. These were the new 'commuters' taking advantage of cheap rail-rides into the city of London to settle in the Home Counties.

Distressed by the destruction of the vernacular cottage in her home county of Surrey, artist Helen Allingham set out to record their rural charms before their inevitable gentrification. In what would become a famous series of watercolours, Allingham painted her houses with such guile and grace that her images came to exemplify the perfect country cottage.

Born in Burton-on-Trent in 1848, Helen Paterson had studied at the Birmingham School of Design and later at the Female School of Art and the Royal Academy, supporting herself by producing illustrations for magazines and books. When she married William Allingham, an Irish poet and editor (she was 25, he 50 and their friends included influential figures like John Ruskin, Alfred Lord Tennyson and Dante Gabriel Rossetti), she devoted herself first to her family and then, when they moved to Sandhills near Witley in Surrey in 1881, to the series of cottage paintings which became her trademark.

She portrayed a tranquil, timeless world where working women were always lovely, the evening sun was always golden and the cottage porch was inevitably wreathed in roses. Allingham, however, not only captured the stuff of fantasy, but also reflected the tail end of a curious debate over the 'correct' appearance of the pretty country cottage and its surrounding landscape. Launched in 1782 by an artistic clergyman, the Revd William Gilpin (who had journeyed down the 'correctly picturesque' River Wye), the picturesque movement was advanced by two Herefordshire neighbours, Uvedale Price and Payne Knight. 'When I consider the striking natural beauties of such a river as that at Matlock, and the effect of the seven-storey buildings that have been raised there . . .

Pictures of rustic homes, such as this one in *Off Marketing* by Helen Allingham, fed people's passion for the perfect country cottage. (*Tom Schaefer*)

for cotton manufactories, I am inclined to think that nothing can equal them for the purpose of disbeautifying an enchanting piece of scenery,' explained Price in his *Essays of the Picturesque* in 1794. In spite of objections ('propriety and convenience are no less objects of good taste than picturesque effects', declared the landscape designer Humphrey Repton in his *Sketches and Hints on Landscape Gardening*, 1795), many landowners embarked on an architectural romp of rustic lodge gates and romantic cottages with thatched gables, eyebrowed dormers and oversized brick chimneys, built not for themselves but for their workers.

The most famous of all the picture postcard villages was Blaize Hamlet near Bristol, built in 1810 by the Quaker banker J.S. Harford

A picture-postcard cottage designed by John Nash, at Blaize Hamlet.

and designed by the architect John Nash. Nash's rustic homes and Allingham's rose-covered cottages inspired a rush of kitsch chocolate-box covers and jigsaw puzzles – and coloured the judgement of all those Edwardian sons and daughters who were marooned in far-flung corners of the British Empire and were destined to fall in love with the idea of the picturesque cottage. As they gazed upon Allingham's reproductions they dreamed of the day when they too might sit out beneath the cottage porch surrounded by the scent of honeysuckle and Albertine roses. The concept of the perfect country cottage had been born.

3

Household Essentials

The Hand-Made Roman Tile

Old clay tiles lend grace and favour to the roofs of village Europe. And just as the finest Havana cigars were said to be those that were hand-rolled on the thigh of the Cuban cigar maker, so too was the original *tuile romaine* formed around the thigh of a Roman tile maker.

Wide at the top and tapered towards the knee, the shape of the *tuile romaine* allowed them to be laid across the roof in undulating, interlocking rows, the narrow neck of each tile gripping the body of the tile above. The weight of the tile, and a gentle roof pitch of 40 to 45 degrees, prevented it, most of the time, from being blown away. The S-shaped profile of the roof, created by the peaks and troughs of the tiles, effectively doubled the surface area of the roof and helped radiate away the summer heat. When the winter rains came the rainwater simply sluiced down the gulleys. The Spanish tile, mission tile, hollow and barrel tile or *tuile à canal* – there were as many regional variations as there were regional names – was a testament to utilitarianism.

The Roman tile sat well on the roofs of the *cabanon* and *mass*, the cottages and farms of lowland Provence, tamed and named Provincia by the Romans around 125 BC. But further north, and high in the Alps

Said to have been shaped around the thigh of a Roman tile maker, the versatile *tuile romaine* could roof a house or, as here, serve as a Breton oyster trap.

and Pyrenees, the *tuile romaine* ran into problems: a persistent wind would drive rain or snow up under the tiles, while a winter gale could strip a roof in minutes. The roofer changed the design, producing a flat or pan tile which could be nailed to the rafters. (When in the sixteenth century the French court decreed that all administrative law would in future be translated from the Latin into the *langue d'oïl* rather than Provençal, the *langue d'oc*, it created a separation of language and culture which is still marked today by the roofs of *tuile romaine* in the south and the roofs of *tuile plat* in the north.)

Where roofing stone was good, cheap and locally available – the Dordogne limestone, for instance, or Breton slate – the clay tile makers made little progress. But being low maintenance, fireproof and sturdy enough to outlive a family generation or two, the clay tiled roof had every advantage over most other roofing materials, including thatch, turf and wooden shingles (a corruption of the German *shindle*, from the Latin *scindula* or *scinod*, meaning to split). Like some medieval double-glazing salesmen, the roof tilers gradually worked their way up through northern Europe, elbowing their business rivals out, until they reached the English Channel.

The sixteenth-century wool trade saw the terracotta tile finally cross into Britain in large quantities. Now found on housing estates from

Canterbury to Carlisle, tiled roofs made their debut on the country houses of the east coast – in Essex, Suffolk, Norfolk, Lincolnshire and Yorkshire – and the west coast county of Somerset after reaching the English wool ports. At first they were carried in as ballast by ships' captains keen to keep an even keel and were simply jettisoned at the port side on arrival. Soon, however, Dutch pantiles were being traded for wool and fine English cloth.

Modern clay tiles line a roof at Mazamet in southern France. Mechanisation of the tile-making process resulted in a product that lacked the charm and grace of the hand-made tile.

Borne inland from the ports along rivers and canals, clay tiles gradually replaced the mouldering thatch of local homes. The wool-rich farmer was unsentimental about tiling over an old thatch roof, especially if he was constantly tripping over chamber pots strategically placed to catch the rainwater dripping through the roof. But rather than construct a new, low-pitched roof to suit the clay tiles, he often laid the tiles on the traditional, steeper pitch of the thatched roof. These curiously steep tiled country roofs remain a familiar feature on the farms and cottages of East Anglia and Somerset today.

The trade in imported roofing tiles eventually attracted local entrepreneurs. At Bridgwater in Somerset, for example, there were sixteen tile and brick works operating within 2 miles of the town bridge by 1850, and here one of the roofing trade favourites, the Bridgwater tile, was born.

Yet in America the clay tile was falling out of favour. Originally imported from Holland, France, Spain and Britain, hand-made clay tiles were manufactured by Dutch settlers in the upper Hudson River Valley and shipped south to New Amsterdam by 1650. The dominant roof tile, the wood shingle, was cheap. However, news of the Great Fire of London in 1666 and another disastrous fire in Boston in 1679 prompted councils to introduce fire codes and substitute the fireproof clay tile in America's towns right through from the 1690s to the 1830s. Then, as fireproof roof materials such as galvanised iron and tinplate became more popular, tile production slumped.

It was another Roman invention, the Italianate villa with its stucco walls and terracotta roof, which rescued the Roman tile. The popular villa revitalised the tiling industry. As metal workers strove unsuccessfully to replicate the ever more popular clay tile in tin, large tile-making works were set up at Akron in Ohio and Baltimore in Maryland. By the 1870s the first roof tile-making machines were being patented and within 20 years production of the hand-made tile – traditionally formed over the tapered section of a log – had dwindled.

Back in Britain in 1905 G.A.T. Middleton reported (in *Building Materials*) that 'the longitudinal bend of an ordinary plain roofing tile is . . . formed by hand over a leather saddle, while any nail holes are punched, also by hand'. The roof tile was still being hand-made – even if it was no longer being fashioned around the Roman craftsman's thigh.

Joseph Aspdin's Cement

In 1850 Mr William Aspdin was planning the construction of a new manor house at the top of Windmill Hill in Gravesend, England. It was not a modest affair. Plans drawn up by a firm of London architects allowed for eleven bedrooms, a picture gallery, dining-room, drawing-room, library, nursery, laundry, breakfast parlour, two kitchens and servants' quarters – not bad for a 34-year-old son of a Leeds bricklayer and his wife Jane, a Barnsley butcher's daughter. The grounds were to be surrounded by a high concrete wall – William Aspdin liked his privacy – and would include lawns, shrubberies, gardens, romantic walks radiating from the mansion and a four-roomed entrance lodge. Most important of all, the building was to be finished in Portland cement stucco and the gardens liberally decorated with statuary cast in Portland cement. And it was to be called Portland Hall, named after the cement invented by his father Joseph Aspdin in 1824.

William Aspdin had significantly (and secretly, to protect the original patent) improved his father's invention and was now, from his bottle kilns at nearby Northfleet, producing barrels of the stuff that would one day swamp the nation's floors in a sea of concrete. Mr Aspdin's cement was to have more of an impact on the average home than any other building material. It promised to make him a very rich man.

The floor of the average town house built between the mid-1800s and early 1900s was made from floorboards clamped together and nailed to joists, the timbers that spanned a room. These joists, from the old French *giste* meaning a couch or bed, were slotted into the walls at either end and rested on brick piers, raising the floor 600mm or so above the ground and creating an air space which allowed fresh air to circulate beneath and keep the damp at bay. (Such floors still function perfectly well in millions of homes today.) The pale pine floorboards were regularly scrubbed clean with a sprinkling of abrasive sand or covered in layer upon layer of thick, dark varnish in an effort to mimic the smart, sombre elm and oak boards of better homes.

For those who could afford neither varnish nor boards, the house builder simply used whatever materials lay close to hand, as house builders have always done. The cheapest was the very earth itself. A universal solution since the beginning of civilisation, an earth floor

One of William Aspdin's original Portland cement-making kilns before it was rescued and restored. (*Lafarge Cement, Chilton*)

was made by mixing the local soil, ideally a good clay, with a moisturiser such as water, skimmed milk or bull's blood, and beating it into a tough, resilient finish with wooden boards or, in Ireland at least, by inviting the neighbours in for a floor-flattening dance. It was, insist those who lived with one, quite as good as any twenty-first-century super-laminated floor.

The ravages of time and hob-nailed boots could be forestalled by reinforcing the floor with small stones and even animal bones. And there was an unexpected and explosive dividend to be had from these porous earth floors. As they absorbed the dirt they produced nitre, used in medicine, dye making and, eventually, gunpowder. When the floors were periodically dug up and replaced with fresh earth, the nitre was sold on as a by-product. As Joseph Aspdin's invention rendered the earth floor redundant the gunpowder men were obliged to find other supplies of nitre.

The Leeds bricklayer Joseph Aspdin had patented his Portland cement after successfully firing pulverised clay and lime in a kiln at between 1300 and 1500°C and then grinding down the clinker to make a particularly strong form of powdered cement. His patent was vague: 'I take a specific quantity of limestone such as that generally used for making and repairing roads . . . but if I cannot procure a sufficient quantity . . . I obtain the limestone itself.' And he took great pains to keep the formula secret, personally supervising the loading of his kilns at Wakefield. His son William would continue the deception when he came to manufacture Portland cement at Rotherhithe: before the kilns were lit he would ostentatiously throw a handful of special powders into the kiln to confuse any commercial spies lurking nearby.

In 1897 scientists curious about the mysterious properties of Portland cement identified its four key compounds while demonstrating a singular lack of originality, naming them alite, belite, celite and felite (dropping the d and e for obvious reasons). But why did the inventor dub it 'Portland' cement?

William Aspdin, son of the inventor of Portland cement. When things went disastrously wrong, he fled his debtors and died in obscurity in Germany.

Joseph Aspdin aimed to improve on the popular brand of the day, Roman cement, which had been patented by James Parker in 1796. It was used not on the house floor but as a stucco finish for brick houses, creating the impression of a superior stone façade. Aspdin needed a name to establish its superiority and the most superior stone of all was the snow-white Portland limestone. Quarried on the Isle of Portland on the English south coast, a million tons were used in the making of Christopher Wren's master-piece, St Paul's Cathedral, while the stonemasons of Virginia shipped it over, block by block, to shape the steps, doorways and window-sills of their clients' fine homes. Naming his cement Portland was a canny and ultimately successful marketing ploy. No mention was made in the patent that John Smeaton had developed his own 'Portland Cement' in 1793 during the construction of a lighthouse on the Eddystone Rocks off Cornwall. Instead, as William Aspdin explained in an advertisement for Portland Cement in 1848, 'its colour so closely resembles that of the stone from which it derives its name as scarcely to be distinguishable from it'.

It was also William who secured a publicity coup and cornered the market for Portland Cement when, having set up the cement works at Rotherhithe in Kent, he met Isambard Kingdom Brunel, who was then engaged on building a tunnel under the Thames. Brunel was persuaded to use Portland – twice the price of Roman cement – after it was successfully employed to repair the tunnel roof. Or so wrote William even as plans progressed for Portland Hall, in this advertisement published in *The Builder* magazine in 1848:

> Portland Cement, solely manufactured by W. Aspdin, son of the patentee. This cement has been proved for upwards of twenty years in the Thames Tunnel to resist the action of water; it is stronger in its cementation qualities, harder and more durable than any other description of cement; it does not vegetate, oxydate or turn green; nor is it affected by any atmospheric influence . . .

Two years later William Aspdin moved his business operation to Gateshead, where labour was cheap and the local Boulder clay plentiful. Here he opened the Patent Portland Cement Works, a building which looked more like a palace than a factory with its parapets, arches, balustrades and urns, topped with a statue of Hercules. 'The buildings are new and spacious and are crowned by a colossal figure of Hercules vainly endeavouring to break upon an anvil a beam of bricks united by the Patent Portland cement of which he is himself made. The whole works have an appearance of symmetry and design very different from those older factories that have arisen . . . in the progress of time and trade,' observed the reporter for the *Newcastle Chronicle*. The Gateshead factory was the largest cement works in the world and, until similar enterprises opened elsewhere, it shipped barrel-loads of Portland cement right across it.

Cement technology was not new. The first records of a concrete floor date back over eight and a half thousand years. The Chinese used concrete on the Great Wall of China and the Romans used it on the Coliseum and the Pantheon in Rome. It was the Romans who perfected the technology and, from their *caementum* and their *concretus*, passed on the terminology. *Concretus*, meaning grown together, referred to the business of mixing sand, small stones and cement and, after adding

Despite Aspdin's death, the Portland cement business prospered. In the early 1900s men in south-east England fill sacks with cement ready for shipping by sailing barge. (*Lafarge Cement, Chilton*)

water, leaving it to set like stone. The magic ingredient in *concretus* was cement, the setting agent which promised to make millions for William Aspdin after the death of his father in 1855.

The Romans already knew how to grind down certain stones and mix the powdered rock with water and grit to make concrete. They knew, too, that the pink volcanic ash at Pozzuoli produced an even stronger cement. Vitruvius provided a recipe for it, recommending one part of *pozzolana* to one part of lime as a sensible mix. Like any building site brickie, the Roman builder liked a mortar that behaved itself, a mortar that slid like butter from the trowel, but was still stiff enough to support a brick or tile. He 'fattened' his mortars with animal fats, blood and even milk. He also discovered that his *concretus* would double in strength if it were drizzled over reinforcing bronze bars.

When two thousand years later Aspdin's 'new' Portland cement arrived on the building site it became the superglue of the century, destined not only to floor the world's homes but to transform its buildings too. The new material had its detractors. Augustus Pugin condemned it and 'a host of other deceptions' because it 'serves to degrade design', but there was no stopping the grey gloop of the cement mixer. In America in 1903 the first concrete high-rise was built in Cincinnati, and in 1908 Thomas Edison built a street of concrete houses at Union, New Jersey. In the same year Britain's first complete concrete high-rise, the Royal Liver Building, rose up in Liverpool. In 1936 British legislators were persuaded to introduce 'model health' by-laws which required all new homes to have a sound and solid concrete floor. This legislation, designed to counter the debilitating effects of damp and deal with a shortage of building lumber, ushered in the new concrete floors which still dominate the domestic market today.

So what of the man who stood to reap the profits from the invention of Portland cement? In the late 1850s everything went disastrously wrong for the entrepreneur William Aspdin. The building of Portland Hall ground to a halt because of unpaid debts and the half-finished mansion was sold. The owner of the Gateshead factory meanwhile took Aspdin to court for non-payment of rent. As the debts piled up Aspdin and his family fled the country for Germany where, after an abortive business venture or two, he slipped and fell in the street of his adopted home, Itzehoe. He died shortly afterwards, aged 48.

Thomas Whitty's Carpet

Oriental kelims, Scandinavian ryas, Greek flokatis and 1960s shag pile: we have been warming our bare feet on woollen rugs and carpets for centuries. But it was thanks to a Devon carpet maker, one Thomas Whitty, born over three hundred years ago, that we have been able to carpet so many square metres of our homes.

Three centuries ago carpets covered tables. The few small carpets imported to Europe from Turkey and Persia were far too precious to be walked upon and were used as furniture covers and wall-hangings instead. The one fabric fit for the average floor was the floor cloth, a piece of plain or painted canvas that was laid across the floorboards or on the bare beaten earth. Made from sailing cloth, it could be cut to fit a room from wall to wall, and thus it was the first fitted carpet. However, it did not stand the commercial test of time, unlike natural fibres which, despite being the most basic of floor coverings, are with us still, marketed in that mysterious language of the IKEA catalogue as Mjang, Klampen and Vasby, but better known as sisal, coir, maize leaf, jute and grass.

Another long-time survivor is the rag rug, a hand-crafted item made by hooking strips of rag through a coarse canvas backing such as an old hessian flour sack. It employed the same basics – a thick, cushioning material woven through a strong, flexible backing – as those used to make one of the earliest known examples of carpet, a 2,500-year-old 'Pazyryk' woven rug, found preserved in the ice of a cave tomb in Outer Mongolia. And it was made using the same technique as that followed by homesteaders in the eighteenth and nineteenth centuries as they turned out their 'turkey-work', hand-made versions of the Turkish carpet.

Yet, despite J.C. Loudon's insistence in 1833 that 'stair carpets give an air of great comfort and finish to a house', few people could yet afford them. Floor cloths, rag rugs made from drapers' remnants or a few small carpet squares economically arranged around the table or bedside was the best most people could manage. Within half a century, however, the carpet was becoming as common as concrete.

The story of its beginnings reads like a history of industrial espionage. One of the early spies in this furtive world of soft furnishings was Henry, 9th Earl of Pembroke. His lordship owned a substantial property in Wiltshire where, according to John Britton's *Beauties of Wiltshire* (1801), 'the first carpet ever made in England was manufactured'. It was made at Wilton, he explained, 'by, and under the directions of one Anthony Duffosy, who is lately dead'. The deceased Mr Duffosy, toiling over this piece of carpet history, had been brought to Wilton from France with another carpet maker, Peter Jemaule, by the earl.

'During his travels in Flanders and France the Earl is said to have taken great interest in the carpet works of these countries,' revealed the *Salisbury and Winchester Journal* in 1884. 'He entered into an arrangement with two Frenchmen, Anthony Duffosy and Peter Jemaule, who are said to have been conveyed to this country in a barrel.' Whether this was an early effort to contravene immigration controls is unclear, but no sooner had the weaving looms of Wilton been improved upon and patented in 1741 than more secret agents were at work.

In 1749, according to the disgruntled Britton, 'some persons at Kidderminster . . . soon procured looms on the same principle with the trifling difference of having bobbin and *ball*, instead of bobbin and *anchor*, and by this means evaded the letter of the law'.

It seemed that nothing about carpets could be kept secret. By the start of the 1800s there were Wiltons and Kidderminsters, Moorfields and Kilmarnocks, Brussels and Venetians, as well as expensive imports from India, Persia and Turkey. As Candace Wheeler pointed out to her American readers later in the century, not all foreign manufacturers were dependable: 'It is true there are bad Oriental rugs, very bad ones, just as there may be a villain in any congregation of the righteous, but certainly the long centuries of Eastern manufacture, reaching back to the infancy of the world, have given Eastern nations secrets not to be easily mastered by the people of later days.'

One weaver who did manage to master the Oriental ways was a Devonshire man, Mr Thomas Whitty. He lived in the small town of

Early fitted carpets. An advertisement for Thomas Whitty's carpets promised to 'undertake to cover the whole of a Room in the compleat manner'. (*Axminster Carpets*)

Axminster and in the 1750s he set about revolutionising the British carpet industry. 'I think it was in the year 1754, that being in London I [saw] . . . one of the best and largest Turkey carpets in England,' Thomas Whitty would recall later. 'After I had seen this carpet, I could never keep it out of my mind long together, without being able to form the least idea of the method of doing it. . . . When I came home, I immediately began to prepare a loom and materials for making a carpet, and on MIDSUMMER-DAY 1755 (a memorable day for my family) I began the first carpet I ever made.'

Whitty wove his carpet, which measured 36 × 21ft (11 × 6.4m), on a specially made upright loom. Even the prestigious Royal Society of Arts wrote to congratulate the little Devon weaver on his achievement. Since the average loom could produce a carpet no more than a metre wide, large carpets had to be made from several strips sewn together. Whitty, meanwhile, continued the laborious business of producing large carpets – so laborious that each completed carpet was ceremoniously taken to Axminster Church for a blessing, the bells ringing out in celebration, before being carted off to its new owners. They were invariably rich. A Whitty original was sold to the owners of Saltram House in Plymouth (and is still to be seen there). In 1790, in a classic case of what the French would call carrying water to the river (and the English taking coals to Newcastle), the Sultan of Turkey, home to the world's finest carpets, was persuaded to buy one of Whitty's Axminsters. The sultan paid a very good price for it: £1,000.

As so often in the history of the house, it was the industrial revolution that powered up production and brought prices tumbling down. In 1791 a carpet factory opened in Philadelphia; in 1801 a new weaving machine revolutionised patterned fabric weaving; and in 1839 the American Erasmus Biglow invented a power loom, which he promptly sold to the English. Five years earlier a British government report condemned the use of 'draw boys' who were 'aroused from their sleep wretched and miserable,

N3. Their price.are 25 per yard fquare for the beft fort, and 15 per yard fquare, for the Common fort. Turkey Patterns at 14 India & Perfia Patterns at 16.

Where once only the wealthy could buy even the 'common sort' of carpet, home-owners can now afford to carpet the whole house. (*Axminster Carpets*)

at two, three or four o'clock'. Their tasks included drawing out the wire over which the carpet pile was formed. The government accused carpet makers of working the draw boys through the night to get the carpets finished – it was blatant child labour, but it helped to nibble away at costs.

Soon the average Victorian and Edwardian villa owner found he could afford to 'close carpet' his reception room, or in other words to buy sufficient carpet to cover the entire floor (although Loudon, for reasons of economy, advised against 'the carpet to be fitted to the room' of the average cottage). The rush to carpet the home came too late for Thomas Whitty and his Axminsters: in 1835, after a disastrous fire, the factory closed. Whitty's machines were sold to his rivals at Wilton and only the Axminster name and technique survived.

And there the Axminster story would have ended had it not been for a chance meeting between a clergyman and a fisherman on a train to Penzance in 1935. The two men fell into conversation and the clergyman asked the fisherman what he did for a living. 'I make Axminster carpets, in Kidderminster,' he replied, introducing himself as Harry Dutfield. What a curious world, mused the cleric, introducing himself as the vicar of Axminster. And how odd that,

Carpet-bagger Harry Dutfield, with a pair of the New Zealand 'carpet master' lambs. He rescued the manufacture of the carpet at Axminster after a chance meeting with a clergyman on a train to Cornwall. (*Axminster Carpets*)

while the world-famous Axminster carpets were made elsewhere, the town itself had lost its carpet industry to the rival Wilton factory exactly a century before.

Harry Dutfield continued on his fishing holiday in a thoughtful mood. The Scots-born son of a carpet designer, Dutfield was as familiar with the business of carpet making as he was with the problems facing the industry: growing foreign competition and a shortage of good quality wool. And yet demand had continued to grow long after the practice of using draw boys had been outlawed. In 1936 Dutfield quit his job at Kidderminster and set about reopening Thomas Whitty's old factory in Axminster.

In 1959 he travelled to New Zealand to inspect the sheep whose fleeces were exported to the Devon factory. The sheep, cross-bred

Kent Romneys famous for the quality of their wool, were good – but not good enough. Working with a New Zealand geneticist, Dr Francis W. Dry, the two men developed a new super breed, the Drysdale or 'carpet master', as the sheep became known. In 1976 Axminster imported its first Drysdale sheep and the 'carpet masters' started a new life grazing the Devon hills.

In 1955 broad looms were brought in that could make a 9 or 12ft wide carpet in a matter of hours rather than days. The introduction from the USA of tufted carpets, based on candlewick weaving techniques, and the use of wool substitutes (although the Drysdale flock continued to provide the essential ingredients for all-wool carpets) finally put the fully fitted carpet within everyone's reach. By the end of the twentieth century more homes in Britain were fitted with carpets than ever before (98 per cent compared with 16 per cent in France or only 2 per cent in Italy). Meanwhile health workers, perplexed by the rising number of allergies, began to question the benefits of the fully fitted carpet. Investigating high levels of infant asthma (the UK had the highest levels of childhood asthma in the world) and adult allergies such as asthma, eczema and hay fever, researchers warned of correspondingly high levels of mite allergens in fitted carpets. Perhaps the fully fitted carpet was not such a good thing after all.

Count Rumford's Chimney

'Now stir the fire, and close the shutters fast,
Let fall the curtains, wheel the sofa round,'

instructed William Cowper in his homily on a winter's evening. For centuries people have been stoking up the fire and staring into the smouldering embers. They were doing so in Jordan at least 10,000 years ago, according to archaeologists who unearthed primitive hearths in the form of small, clay-lined depressions in the floors of village homes. For centuries they did so without the benefit of a decent chimney.

The traditional *tigh dubh*, or black house, of the Outer Hebrides was said to be named after its smoke-blackened interior. The *tigh dubh* was built with a double skin of stone, the cavities between filled with an insulating layer of earth or peat. A roof thatch of marram grass was held in place by fishing ropes weighed down with rocks and the early black house boasted no chimney. Instead the swirling peat smoke was allowed to curl its way around the open rafters before finding a way out through a rudimentary hole in the roof.

This lack of a proper chimney had been causing problems back in the 1500s, according to the satirist Bishop Joseph Hall who wrote in 1625 of the average farmhouse

> . . . whose thatched spars are furred with sluttish soote
> A whole inch thick, shining like a blackmoor's brows,
> Through the smoke that down the headlesse barrel blows.

The smoky interiors were a hazard to health. 'The plague of a smoking chimney is proverbial,' wrote Benjamin Thompson in the

John Leech illustrates the adverse effect of the smoking chimney. (*Punch*)

1790s. And, he warned, these old-fashioned fires presented other dangers. 'Those cold and chilling draughts of air on one side of the body while the other side is scorched by a chimney fire, . . . cannot but be highly detrimental to health.' The effects on those of a weak constitution, he thought, could be fatal: 'I have not a doubt in my own mind that thousands die in this country every year of consumptions occasioned solely by this cause.' Yet it was a cause 'so easily removed!' he declared. Benjamin Thompson, or Count Rumford as he became, was the man to do it.

Thompson was born in 1753 in a cottage in Woburn, Massachusetts, the home of a family of British loyalists. By the age of 19 he had found a wealthy wife nearly twenty years his senior and employment as a schoolmaster. Four years later, as the US Congress adopted the Declaration of Independence, he abandoned his wife and their two-year-old daughter and fled to England when it became apparent that he had been spying on the Americans for the British.

Thompson never returned to America. Instead he earned a knighthood from the British authorities for his scientific work (via some influential political connections) before moving to Bavaria where, having reformed the military and introduced workhouses for the poor, he was awarded the title of count. Unknown to the Bavarian court, their hero was busily passing information about the country back to Britain. He adopted the name Rumford after the New Hampshire town where he had abandoned his wife, and returned to London in his 40s with a new passion: to cure the smoking chimney.

Rumford acquired his knowledge of 'Fire-places for burning Coals, or Wood, in an open Chimney' from careful observation. 'Things near us . . . are seldom objects of our meditations. How few persons are there who ever took the trouble to bestow a thought on the subject in question, though it is, in the highest degree, curious and interesting?' he asked. By investigating the inefficiencies of the conventional fireplace and flue Rumford was able to 'cure' the smoking chimneys at several eminent London residences. Sixteenth-century celebrities such as Lord Palmerston, Sir Joseph Banks, Sir John Sinclair and Lady Templeton ('and a great many others; but it would be tiresome to enumerate on them all,' said Rumford modestly) all benefited from his attention. Not only were they saved from the effects of the smoking chimney, they also gained from 'the saving of fuel, arising from these improvements [which] amounts in all cases to more than half, and in many cases to more than two-thirds of the quantity formerly consumed,' he claimed.

Sir John Sinclair was prepared to provide a gratifying testimonial: 'You will hear with pleasure that your mode of altering chimnies [*sic*] so as to prevent them smoking, to save fuel and to augment heat, has answered not only with me, but with many friends,' he wrote to the count.

It would be another century before the British flue was fully 'Rumfordised'. However, recommendations such as these helped persuade President Jefferson to equip his estate at Monticello in Virginia with Rumford fireplaces designed to burn wood instead of coal. Henry David Thoreau, who took to a cabin in the woods near Concord, Massachusetts, in the 1840s to pen his philosophical classic *Walden, or Life in the Woods*, declared that the Rumford fireplace was one of those modern conveniences which too many people took for granted.

Rumford's radical designs were adopted across the industry and, even now, two centuries later, the tall, narrow Rumford fireplace remains on the market. What was the man's secret? He insisted on streamlining the throat – 'I mean the lower extremity of its canal; the best width is 4 inches' – and splaying the fireplace so as to radiate heat back into the room and avoid 'those accidental puffs of smoke which are sometimes thrown into rooms by the carelessness of servants in putting on suddenly too many coals'. He promised: 'When the alterations proposed are properly executed, the chimneys will never fail to answer.'

After being 'Rumfordised', chimneys such as these at Wells in Somerset were guaranteed to be more efficient.

In a final essay on improving the fireplace, Rumford inadvertently touched on the business of child labour, a scandal that would not be properly exposed and legislated against until the late 1800s. 'Provision must be made for the passage of the chimney-sweeper up the chimney,' he wrote. 'In building up the new back of the fireplace . . . an opening . . . 11 or 12 inches wide, must be begun in the middle of the back, and continued to the top of it.' This, he explained, would create an opening 'about 12 to 14 inches' high and 'quite sufficient to allow the chimney-sweeper to pass'. (Not until 1834 was legislation introduced forbidding boys under 10 years old from working as chimney sweeps, but even then the law was largely ignored.)

The eccentric count (he wore his habitual, all-white winter attire, he once explained, for thermal rather than fashionable reasons) married a Parisian widow in 1805 and died in Paris in 1814. Although President Roosevelt would later rank him as one of the greatest minds America ever produced, along with Thomas Jefferson and Benjamin Franklin, for the most part he became another forgotten hero of the house.

God's Best Boiler

In 200 BC a Greek named Hero devised a novelty steam-driven toy. His *aelopile*, a hollow sphere set above a cauldron, spun round furiously on its axis as the fire beneath turned the water in the cauldron to steam. It took two millennia to translate Hero's invention into a device that would make redundant all the hard work of heating a home: splitting logs, carrying coal, cleaning out the ash and sweeping the chimneys. This long and circuitous route to full central heating had started with the simple concept of heating water in a container. In a modern world of digital displays and computer chip technology, it is comforting that the down-to-earth name for this sophisticated device survives: the boiler.

The history of its progress from Hellenic plaything to the heating unit which has a place in virtually every new home built since the 1950s is marked by famous, and not so famous, people. In 1680 a Frenchman, Dr Denis Papin, invented a steam digester for food processing. On this machine he installed the first recorded safety valve. In 1698 Thomas Savery constructed the first commercially successful steam engine which could pump water (in the process instigating the technology that would power the industrial revolution).

In America the business of boilering helped pioneer patent law. When William Blakely wished to register his patent for an

House Tax

Governments have been successfully making money out of people's houses for centuries. One unpopular tax on British homes (was any tax ever popular?) was hearth money, a tax of 2 shillings per hearth, paid twice yearly to the English Exchequer from 1662. This tax was repealed during the Glorious Revolution of 1688 on the grounds that it allowed the revenue men to search taxpayers' homes.

There were other ways of raising revenue from the house. There was the English wallpaper tax, for example, a double duty charged on paper that was hand-coloured for use on walls. The excise men laboriously stamped their duty paid mark on every yard of wallpaper produced until the duty was lifted in 1836.

In the 1600s the practice of 'clipping' silver coins (the silver parings were melted down and sold on) was roundly condemned by the wealthy who resented this literal devaluing of their currency. To defray the costs, the Exchequer introduced a

Tax dodge! A Bath householder tries it on with the tax man. Two windows placed less than 12 inches apart were eligible for two-for-one tax relief.

window tax in 1697. Houses worth more than £5 a year and with more than six windows (excepting the dairy) were taxed accordingly. From the Exchequer's point of view it was a thorough success: the tax was increased six times between 1747 and 1808 and only abolished 154 years later when London's Crystal Palace was built. From the taxpayer's point of view it was a burden which fell mainly on the middle classes: one Lincoln curate, the Revd John Williams, paid 13 shillings in window tax over and above his rent of £7 11*s* 4*d* in 1751. When William Pitt's government raised the 'tax on light' in 1784 a householder in Bath etched the following words on his window-pane:

> God gave us light, and it was good.
> Pitt came and taxed it, damn his blood.

To avoid the tax, home-owners blocked up windows or shuffled two together to benefit from a two-for-the-price-of-one tax relief: if two windows were closer together than 12 inches they were taxed as a single window. The result, complained the *Bath Chronicle* of 1851, was a 'debased, blinded architecture. Sham windows, borrowed lights, and palpable contrivances to cheat the Exchequer, everywhere stare us in the face.'

It was no better elsewhere in Europe. In seventeenth-century Spain a law was passed requiring owners of two-storey houses to place half their home and its furniture at the disposal of the Spanish court. The royal family regularly travelled with a retinue of up to 300 in waiting and a further 500 serving men. When the court moved to Valladolid in central Spain, it was noted that many householders in Castilla y León had built single-storey homes to evade the hospitality tax. Such homes were dubbed *Casa de la Malicia*, literally the houses of wickedness, and were roundly condemned by the court until eventually the law was repealed.

A broken boiler caused domestic misery. It was dangerous, too. In 1880 over 250 Americans were killed by exploding boilers.

improvement on Savery's engine, he had to take the slow boat to England in 1766 to do so. When John Stevens came to register his own improvement (his steam engine did not warm any homes, but it did power a Hudson riverboat in 1803), he was damned if he was going to travel all the way to England to register ownership of the idea. Instead he successfully petitioned the US Congress to introduce patent law in 1790.

By the early part of the nineteenth century the American Solomon Willard, who had worked with the architect Isaiah Rogers, developed a central heating system which was used to heat the public rooms and halls of at least one New York mansion by the 1830s. But even with Papin's safety valve, boiler work was a notoriously dangerous business. Charles Dickens made a jocular

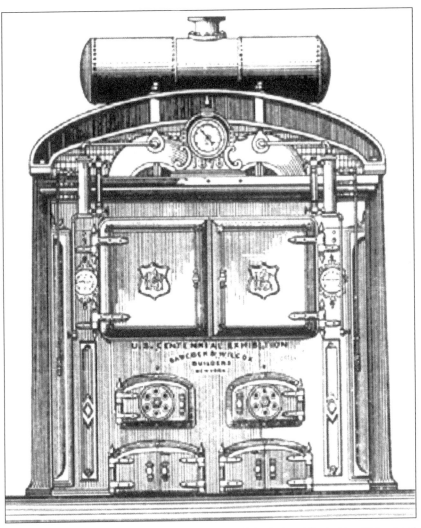

Babcock and Wilson's patent safety boiler saved lives . . . and helped reform US patent law. (*Babcock and Wilson Company*)

reference to 'bursting boilers' in *The Pickwick Papers*, while the Revd Francis Kilvert, taking a sneaky tour around Claremont House in Surrey (he was acquainted with one of the staff), noted in 1870: 'In the back kitchen a boiler had just burst and the ruin of the boiler was standing surrounded by debris.' Standing anywhere near a bursting boiler could be fatal. The trade magazine *Steam* reported that in 170 boiler explosions recorded in America in 1880 259 people were killed and another 555 injured.

The credit for making boilers safer, especially big industrial ones, goes to Stephen Wilson of Rhode Island, USA, who patented his safety water tube boiler in 1856. Eleven years later he teamed up with George Babcock to develop and market the new, 'non-explosive boiler'. Babcock and Wilson boilers heralded the age of the city, their big boilers producing the electricity required to power up the street lights, first in Philadelphia in 1881 and then in New York's famous Pearl Street Central station a year later. When Thomas Edison installed a Babcock and Wilson heating boiler in his own laboratory in 1888 he declared it 'the best boiler God has permitted man yet to make'.

It would be some years before the technology improved the lives of most people (for whom a boiler was an old hen fit only for the pot). In England, while the likes of Lord Derby had been using a rudimentary central heating system with a boiler and hot water pipes to warm his conservatory since 1817, the average householder endured the cold with the fortitude of a Christmas morning bather.

> I sat down in my bath upon a sheet of thick ice which broke in the middle into large pieces whilst sharp points and jagged edges stuck all round the sides of the tub like chevaux de frise, not particularly comforting to the naked thighs and loins, for the keen ice cut like broken glass. The ice water stung and scorched like fire. I had

Punch cartoonist John Leech lampoons domestic heating arrangements in nineteenth-century England. (*Punch*)

to collect the floating pieces of ice and pile them on a chair before I could use the sponge and then I had to thaw the sponge in my hands for it was a mass of ice.

The Revd Francis Kilvert was preparing for his winter morning service in 1870. 'The Church was very cold in spite of two roaring stove fires.'

Curiously all the inventing needed to bring central heating to the shire rectories had already been accomplished. A central heating system based on Hero's *aelopile* required a heat source (the boiler), a pump to propel the hot water around the pipework, and radiators to spread the heat into the room. Jacob Perkins had devised small-bore continuous pipe as early as 1832, and the Busby patent circulator had been invented around the same time.

Yet when architect E.C. Morgan Willmott published his plans for a modern, five-bedroomed country doctor's house 'with a Motor-house attached' in 1908 – 'the estimated cost is £1,200' – he included a consulting room, waiting room, dispensary and no fewer than ten fireplaces. '*Well* fires, or others of a similar nature, are the best for heating purposes, burning as they do little coal, and giving great heat.' But Morgan Willmott was about to be proved wrong. In the same year that he published his plans the Ideal company began importing cast-iron boilers and radiators to Britain from America. Given their weight, it would take several grunting men to move, let alone install, them. Nevertheless this marked the dawn of domestic central heating and gradually the weight, size and, more importantly, cost of the boilers came down.

George and Thomas Baxendale, whose father had founded a manufacturing business making 'railway wagons . . . gip wagons, trains for general purposes, colliery pit boxes, wheels and axles complete' at Chorley in Lancashire, diversified into the manufacture of 'kitchen ranges, Bakers' and Confectioners' Ovens' in the early 1900s. After the Second World War, as central heating became something worth saving up for, Baxendale started making back boilers, small, high-output water heaters linked to the living-room coal fire and capable of heating several radiators. The Baxi boiler was to become the Vauxhall Victor of the plumbing world: cheap and reliable. As house coal was edged out in favour of gas, the Baxendales launched the Baxi Bermuda at Park Lane in London in 1966. The Bermuda was a conventional living-room gas fire with a boiler fitted behind to provide hot water and heat several radiators. It was a sturdy little design, and 30 years later home-owners were still buying nearly 2.5 million Bermudas a year.

Baxendales were just one of a host of boiler makers. Another, started by plumber Thomas Potterton in the nineteenth century,

It might have become a 'unit', but the central heating system still relied on the basic boiler. (*Worcester Bosch*)

The Air Conditioner

An American called Willis Haviland Carrier invented the means to keep a house cool. He had not intended to do so. In 1924 his company had installed three industrial chiller units to help keep stock cool at the J.L. Hudson department store, in Detroit, Michigan. When store managers reported unusually high sales from customers who clearly enjoyed chilling out in the store, Carrier wondered if his 'apparatus for treating air' might have a domestic application. When the New York's Rivoli Theatre boosted summer film audiences by installing a unit and advertising the cool comforts of its 'air-conditioned auditorium', Carrier began to appreciate the full potential of the household market. His Weathermaker air conditioner was introduced in 1928 and finally, in the years after the Second World War, sales took off. (By 2003 air conditioning was the single largest energy user in the buildings of Florida, consuming upwards of 45 per cent of the state's power.)

Natural air conditioning. Until Carrier's invention the verandah was the simple solution to keeping cool at home.

Carrier had started out by stabilising air temperatures at a Brooklyn printing works where fluctuations of heat and humidity had been adversely affecting the printing process. In 1906 he patented his 'apparatus for treating air'. Carrier did not invent 'air conditioning', a process which, strictly speaking, refers to the business of conditioning yarn with water vapour in a textile plant, and was invented by engineer Stuart H. Cramer. But, in what Carrier later called a flash of genius, he did resolve the problems of temperature, humidity control and dew-point while he sat waiting for a train one foggy night in 1911.

Having set up the Carrier Engineering Corporation in 1915, Carrier patented a centrifugal refrigeration machine in 1921 and concentrated on its commercial applications until customers in downtown Detroit persuaded him otherwise. Nearly a century later Carrier's original formula, devised on that misty station platform, still forms the basis for the fundamental calculations of the air-conditioning industry.

A boy provided the air conditioning in this Indian Army bungalow, by pulling a string attached to the ceiling curtain.

eventually took over the Baxi business, but the Baxi Bermuda remained a very public success. The perennial complaint of visitors to Britain in the 1960s, apart from the food, was that British homes were always cold: not surprising when in 1960 only 5 per cent of them had central heating. A decade later 55 per cent of homes had central heating: the Baxi boiler had won them over.

In the 1930s the average housewife spent just under an hour and a half every day tending the fires: central heating dispensed with the lot and rendered redundant all the apparatus of the open fire from gridirons, fire-backs and chimney-cranes to kettle tilters, idlebacks and handymaids (devices for tilting a hot kettle from a fire). And yet old favourites die hard: a survey of Americans in the 1990s, reported by Terence Conran in the *Essential House Book*, found that 90 per cent of those questioned wanted a fireplace in their home – even if they lived in a place which was warm all year round.

4

House Works

Men of Glass

The following notice was hung from the railings outside the Duke of Wellington's home in 1839: 'Those desirous of seeing the interior of the house are requested to ring at the door of entrance and express their desire. It is wished that the practice of stopping on the paved walk to look in at the windows should be discontinued.'

We look through windows and we see the world outside (or in the duke's case, inside). We tend to forget the glass itself, an extraordinary material with an extraordinary history. According to Pliny the Elder, glass making started the day traders landed a ship in Syria to prepare a meal on the beach. 'There were no stones to support their cooking-pot, so they placed lumps of soda under them. When these became hot and fused with the sand on the beach, streams of an unknown translucent liquid flowed, and this is the origin of glass.'

In the nineteenth century whenever anyone died in his or her cottage home in North Wales a pane of glass in the cottage window was ritually broken. Only then could the deceased's soul escape from the house. The shattering of the glass was a considerable sacrifice. In poorer homes a glazed window was such an expensive commodity that casements were often listed in wills as an inheritable fitting, rather than a fixture, of the home.

Most glass, however, was coarse, thick, uneven and only semi-transparent. Broadsheet or muff glass, as it was known, was made when the glass blower dipped his pipe, or iron, into the glory hole, the heart of the furnace, and blew out a globe from the lump of molten glass. The hot globe was swung like a pendulum until it formed a drooping cylinder that could be cut open with shears by the glass blower's assistant. This sheet was then laid out flat on a metal plate ready to be cut into panes.

The rippled irregularities and imperfections in broadsheet glass were created when it came into contact with the metal plate. By contrast Normandy, or crown, glass, which did not come into contact with any surface while molten, was brilliantly clear. If muff glass was for the tenant, crown glass was for his landlord. There were alternatives for those who could afford neither: 'Of old time our country houses instead of glass did use much lattice and that made either of wicker or fine rifts of oak in checkerwise. I read also that some . . . did make panels of horns instead of glass,' noted William Harrison in his 1577 *Description of England*.

Much of the early English crown glass was made at London's Bear Garden Glasshouse in Southwark, owned by the Duke of Buckingham, after whose coronet or 'crown' the glass was named. The method of manufacture, which had crossed over to England from Normandy, involved spinning or 'flashing' a globe of molten glass on a rod or pontil until the centrifugal force formed a perfect circular plate 1.5m across yet as little as 2.8mm thick.

This table of glass could be cut into rectangular panes, graded into firsts, seconds and thirds, the central punty mark or bull's-eye, where the glass had been held against the pontil, being sold off cheap. The fake bull's-eye window-panes on mock Dickensian inns have genuine historical antecedents: the originals were not only inexpensive, they were also less likely to be broken in a bar-room

The punty mark or bull's-eye was a cheap pane of glass, often thrown back into the pot during the manufacture of crown glass.

brawl. The main disadvantage of crown glass was the limited size of panes that could be cut from a single plate. The largest was 560 × 360mm (22 × 14.5in), but most were cut to fit the conventional six by six sash windows (with six panes in the top sash and six below). The smallest panes were reserved for the traditional leaded casement windows.

Early plate-glass makers pour molten glass onto a table while those to their right roll the glass out into a plate. (*Pilkington plc*)

All this changed when Robert Lucas Chance, a man who could turn an old trick into a new enterprise, entered the scene. Lucas joined his father's business at the age of 12. At 14 the 'little master in the jacket', as he was known, assumed charge of the warehouse. By 1804 he was a full partner. When Sarah, his mother, died in 1809, his father William was inconsolable. William wrote of his wife's funeral: 'Myself not attended for want methinks of fortitude.' He lost interest in the business and Lucas Chance took control.

In 1810, leaving his younger brother William in charge of the Birmingham works, Lucas took over the ailing Nailsea glassworks in London and, with the help of a crown glass expert, John Hartley from Dumbarton, turned it into a successful enterprise. Lucas moved his young family down to London, at first to a house in Gower Street and then, as profits permitted, to a smarter house with a large garden at Highgate Hill. The busy Mr Chance had little time for gardening. Said to take his meals while walking so that he could exercise as he ate, Chance next bought up a glassworks at Smethwick in the West Midlands in 1824, turning it into Chance Brothers Glassworks.

In 1832, after a trip to Europe, Lucas Chance introduced new blood and radical new ideas to his Birmingham factory. The new blood was provided by French and Belgian workers who could turn out 'improved cylinder glass'. As with the old muff glass, workers still swung molten glass into a cylinder, but the new technique produced a superior glass that is still to be found in the windows of period homes today. G.A.T. Middleton described its character in 1915: 'The better qualities [are] perfectly flat with few bubbles, and the lower qualities with a wavy surface distorting objects seen through it, and containing long, narrow bubbles.' Middleton also described the process, little changed in eighty years: 'Fireclay pots are ranged along the sides of the furnaces . . . with platforms raised some 7ft above the bottom of a pit, so that the blower, standing on the platform, may have a space below him in which to swing his blow-pipe.' Taking a lump of hot glass 'about 20 pounds' on the end of his pipe, he worked it into a cylinder 1145mm (45in) long. 'The top is now cut off, and the cylinder (or "muff") which is thus formed is allowed to cool, and is then cut from end to end. This is put on the stone floor of a flattening oven with the split side upwards, and gradually heated, when it opens out by itself to a flat sheet.'

New glass meant new windows (especially with the lifting of the excise duty on glass in 1845) and the large panes made available by the sheet-glass process transformed the house window market almost overnight. Chance advertised it as 'British sheet-glass . . .

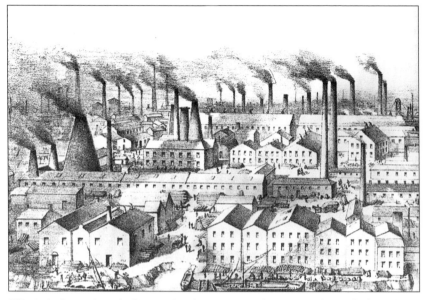

Pilkington's glass works and collieries at St Helens in 1879. Within ten years the British glass rush was jeopardised by the mechanisation of glass making in America. (*Pilkington plc*)

double the substance of Crown Glass'. The old 'six over six' sash windows were replaced with 'two over twos' and later with a single pane above and below. The glass could even be cut into 1245mm (49in) long panes and in 1850 almost a million sheets glazed that new wonder of the Victorian age, the Crystal Palace, home of the Great Exhibition of 1851.

Lucas Chance died in 1865. By now three companies supplied the glass for most British homes and many of those abroad, including America: Chance, their northern rivals Hartley of Sunderland, and a new firm founded in north-west England as the St Helens Crown Glass Company. This upstart outfit relied on the technical expertise of its glass maker John William Bell and the business capital raised by three local families, the Bromilows, the Greenalls and the

Pilkingtons, whose name would become much better known in the next century. Having abandoning his medical career Dr Pilkington had done very well out of a wine and spirit business. There was capital to spare and his son William was prepared to invest it in glass.

For a while it looked like an unwise investment: although Pilkington, Chance and Hartley controlled three-quarters of the market for house glass, problems loomed. Londoners had switched to buying cheaper Belgian glass towards the end of the 1800s. By the 1890s glass makers in America had mechanised the cylinder sheet-glass process and

William Pilkington invested his father's spare capital in a family firm that would eventually dominate the world of glass. (*Pilkington plc*)

American home-owners were sourcing their glass from a self-sufficient market rather than importing from Britain. The glass market in Britain was starting to shatter.

By 1903 Pilkington's was the last British producer left which could provide a sheet-glass replacement for a broken window. Chance and Hartley had both foundered while Pilkington survived not on window glass but by competing with French glass makers for the plate-glass market. By now Edwardian shopkeepers were putting in new plate-glass frontages and public houses were lining their bars with vast sheets of mirrored plate-glass. The barmaid who stands waiting to take orders in Édouard Manet's *A Bar at the Folies-Bergère*

109

(1881) is reflected in the café mirror, a great sheet of French plate glass and a testament to her countrymen's expertise as plate-glass makers. They could manufacture much larger plates of glass than the sheet-glass manufacturers, and, after the arduous business of grinding and polishing the plate-glass sheets by hand, produce glass with a lustre that sheet-glass lacked. The process was still expensive – as far back as the 1730s William Salmon had estimated that it cost £5 to glaze a 6 × 3ft sash window with plate glass, while a glazier working in crown glass could do the job for 18 shillings – but costs were falling and Pilkington branched out into the trade. Pilkington also planned to stake a glazier's claim on household windows across the world and the little company from St Helens was soon sending its salesmen out to set up shop in Montreal, Vancouver, Calgary and Winnipeg as well as Australia, New Zealand and South Africa.

In Britain in the 1920s homes were being built. Lots of homes. The burgeoning middle class, falling interest rates, the spread of the building societies which loaned money to new home-owners, and subsidised council house building allowed the great glass maker to weather the Depression. Even the troubled times of the Second World War did not halt the demand for this, the most fragile of building materials, as a new bombing technique, the *blitzkrieg*, meant Pilkington could claim to have 'twice reglazed London' in the 1940s. Then in the early 1950s Alastair Pilkington conceived the clever idea of forming glass by floating the melted raw materials at high temperature over a bath of molten tin. This new 'float' glass lacked the twinkling imperfections of the old crown glass or the distinctive swirls and eddies of sheet glass, and for the second time in a century the market for house glass was revolutionised. When Alastair Pilkington died in 1995 his float glass was glazing windows across the globe. From the fused sand on a Syrian beach to a float-glass empire, glass had undergone a remarkable transformation.

The Sliding Sash

The sash window is perhaps the most successful accessory our homes have ever had. What started out as a fashionable upgrade for posh houses around 1685 had usurped the alternative casement windows in almost every new home by the late 1800s. 'A very sweete House and Garden and Grounds, it was of brick work coyn'd with stone and the Windows with stone all sashes,' observed Celia Fiennes of one house on her travels in 1697. The indomitable Fiennes travelled all over Britain between 1685 and 1703, paying particular attention to her surroundings and recording in her diary such details as these sash windows. On another occasion she noted a house with 'double sashes to make the house warmer for it stands pretty bleake'. She had spotted a window where both top and bottom sash could be opened: on earlier designs only the bottom sash lifted, to be held open with a wedge or peg.

Early windows let in a little light – and plenty of draughts.

Fiennes would also have seen the sash window adopted in the close streets of the city, the builders proudly setting their new windows flush with the face of the building. It could be a risky business: fire in one house often spread across a street from wooden window to wooden window. In 1709 legislation was introduced to have all such windows set back 500mm.

The heyday for the sash window was the Georgian era, and from 1714 to 1837 the proportions of the windows gave these buildings their poise and elegance. Symmetry was all. On the smart first-floor viewing deck of the Georgian house the dining-room and parlour windows were sometimes made twice as high as they were wide, and the width of the windows on the floors above was gradually reduced until, in the mean servants' quarters at the top of the house, the under-maid's face, when she looked out on the street below, would be framed by a small square of window. On other Georgian houses each sash in each window was constructed as a perfect square so that it matched the larger square created by the placing of the windows on the two principal floors.

The sashes themselves, named from the French *chassis* meaning frame, were a tribute to the skill of the joiners who, as they served out their customary seven-year apprenticeship, constructed the frames at their work benches. On early windows the glazing bars, or astragals, were solid, chunky affairs made from imported Baltic pine. By the close of the eighteenth century they had evolved into more graceful forms with poetic-sounding mouldings like astragal and hollow, sash ovolo and lamb's tongue. The clatter of Victorian mass-production machinery saw the size of glazing bars reduced even further while the small Georgian panes were replaced with larger expanses of glass. The weight of the extra glass strained the construction of the upper sashes with their now relatively slender bottom rails. To compensate, the side stiles were strengthened by lengthening them to form the distinctive horns on either side which appeared on sash windows from around 1840.

Come the fashionable Victorian Gothic revival and the old sash window was dressed up with ornate surrounds, lancet arches, decorative glazing bars and coloured glass. The constant innovation of the age finally saw the thicker glazing bars of the early Georgian style return in a Queen Anne revival style.

By now the sash window had totally eclipsed the casement window with its cumbersome and draughty leaded lights. 'We do not like latticed windows because they are generally cold and gloomy,' wrote J.C. Loudon, though conceding that, 'as they are much cheaper than sashes hung with cords and pulleys, where economy is the main object, recourse must be had to them.' Yet even the dingy interiors of some of the poorest terraced homes were lit by sash windows (although many did not actually open – an opening sash was considered an unnecessary luxury for the labouring classes).

The sliding sash, complete with hanging net curtains, is the most successful accessory our homes have ever had.

Wooden sash windows still grace our town and country houses today, fortunate survivors first of the wave of twentieth-century metal casements and then, in the latter half of the twentieth century, of the blight of white plastic or uPVC frames. But where did the design for the sash originate? Who built the first?

In sixteenth-century Britain there was a fashion for all things Dutch. The intimate domestic scenes of home life in Holland,

Cheap and cheerful. The casement window, seen here on a house in Slovakia, was an economical alternative to the sliding sash window.

painted by artists of the period like Vermeer, marked the beginnings of the private, practical and serviceable home that we celebrate to this day. The fashion reached the peak of chic in the seventeenth century and the sliding sash was almost certainly among the stylish imports. Yet as early as 1519 William Horman was already noting in his *Vulgarium* a house with 'many pretty wyndowes shette with louys goynge up and downe'. Was this the earliest recorded reference to the sash window in Britain? And did this suggest the sash window was devised by some medieval do-it-yourself enthusiast applying some fenestration to his old shutters?

Windows and shutters had developed together, so closely in fact that the terminology itself became confused. The fourteenth-century *fenestrae* referred to the shutters, but came to be translated, in the French *fenestre* and Welsh *ffenestre*, as the name of the window instead. In some early American windows, carried over by settlers from the home country, only the upper half of the window was glazed, the lower half being closed by a wooden shutter. This lower shutter, set in a pair of rails, was raised like a guillotine to provide a little natural ventilation, and it would have been but a short step to replace the shutter with a glazed sash instead.

Then again the sash window may have been a home-grown, English affair. In Yorkshire and elsewhere in the north of England yeomen had been using sash windows rather than casements since at least the early 1700s. Although the Yorkshire sash operated on the horizontal rather than the vertical plain, the essential elements were the same. So who takes credit for the first sash windows? A Dutchman, an American settler or a Yorkshireman? We will never know.

A Question of Ascent

Aside from ensuring that the carpet runner matches the colour of the hall wall, home-owners tend to overlook their stairs. It is an indifference that harks back to utilitarian medieval times when style and design were as remote as fridge-freezers and foam-filled furniture. It is also because there were no heroes of the staircase, no breakthrough inventors or ground-breaking innovators. Every step forward in the development of building materials – stone, timber, iron, concrete and glass – had its parallel step upwards in the development of the stairs.

The staircase has evolved through the centuries simply, sensibly and quietly. Architects played an occasional starring role. Charles Édouard Jeanneret, more popularly known as Le Corbusier, designed a soaring swoop of stairs at the Villa Savoye in the late 1920s, described by one commentator, Eva Jiricna, as 'sophisticated perfection'. Jiricna described another stairway, Oscar Niemeyer's

The Disposable Window

In the latter half of the twentieth century home-owners indulged a passion for home improvement. Double-glazing consistently came top of the list as people paid to have their old (sometimes 150 years old) wooden-framed windows replaced with PVC and later uPVC frames. Plastics had turned the window frame into a disposable item. But by the turn of the twenty-first century an estimated 200,000 tonnes of waste a year, created solely by old window frames, was fast filling up British landfill sites as an estimated seven million windows a year were replaced with uPVC.

The industry claimed its product would last forty years; many observers thought that a decade was more realistic. The proponents of uPVC extolled the virtues of a window frame

Indispensable: the wooden-framed window.

that was draughtproof and never needed painting. Its opponents retorted that plastic could never replicate the delicate joinery of seasoned wood. The Irish Georgian Society condemned them, while the Society for the Protection of Ancient Buildings (SPAB) warned that uPVC windows represented 'the home improvement likely to cause most harm to a property's value'. Many home-owners might have done well to heed the sensible words of SPAB's founder, William Morris. He had founded the society in 1877 to counteract the destructive 'restoration' of medieval buildings by Victorian architects, pleading with them to 'show no pretence of the art, and otherwise to resist tampering with either the fabric or ornament of the building as it stands'.

Windows with uPVC frames may be watertight and waterproof, but their coarse lines do not improve the look of this old limestone cottage.

1958 staircase for the Itamaraty Palace in Brasilia, as 'technologically and architecturally magnificent', although the lack of a handrail also made it something of a dangerous liability.

The earliest stairs rose as a series of solid, carved timber platforms, but it was not long before steps were attached to the sloping rail, or string, of the staircase and handrails and balusters were added to prevent the young, old or inebriate from falling off.

The most radical staircase architect – and England's most fashionable one in the 1730s and 1740s – was William Kent, who broke the mould by building a sweep of marble steps in the centre of his client's new home in 1734. The client was Lord Burlington and the house was Holkham Hall, and the idea for the grand staircase (a significant departure from the usual practice of placing it up the side of the building) was inspired by Vitruvius's designs for an Egyptian hall. Ideas like these, employed on the manor and mansion, were soon filtering down through the social orders and before long the look of the average country farmhouse was changing. The medieval hall house, open to the rafters and warmed (heated would be too strong a word) by a smouldering log fire set on the floor, was a place of chaotic companionability. The lord, his lady and their guests would seat themselves on chairs (as opposed to the commoners' stools) on a dais, looking down on a floor 'commonly of clay, strewn with rushes under which lies undisturbed an ancient collection of beer, grease, fragments, bones, spittle, excrement of dogs and cats and everything that is nasty,' according to a letter written by the scholar Erasmus in 1520.

But by Tudor times the great open hall was being partitioned off for privacy. (Not everyone approved: 'The hall has come to a pretty pass when the lord and lady avoid it at mealtimes, dining every day in a private parlour to get away from the poor people,' complained the fourteenth-century poet William Langland.) As the upper half of the hall was floored, and flues were built to take the hearth smoke away through a chimney, instead of through a rudimentary hole in the roof, a ladder or *stee* was used to give access from the ground floor to the bed chamber or *chaamer*. English home-owners, still influenced by the imported designs of their Norman conquerors, sometimes built a flight of stone steps outside the building to the upper chamber, or built the stairs into an outside tower; others, squeezed for space and money, set the great inglenook fireplace in a gable wall and placed a winding stair up around it. Spiral staircases with steps radiating out from a newel post had other uses: the Scots described them as turnpikes and recognised their defensive role in hand-to-hand combat. A good swordsman could grip the newel with one hand and slice at his attackers below with his other, putting the attacker at an unfortunate disadvantage.

The pattern set by Kent was repeated by the Georgian house builder. For here, in the centre of the home, the staircase gave the house a clear, definable sense of symmetry. In the fine new houses of the Georgian age fireplaces were placed to one side of the house, on the gable end, and the staircase, a graceful apparition designed to impress the visitor when they first set foot in the hall, was built in the centre of the house facing the door.

The *piano nobile*, the 'noble floor', was the place for greeting and entertaining guests, high above the steamy kitchen quarters and sufficiently elevated above the common pavement outside. A short but elegant flight of steps was all that was needed to provide the SUV effect – that sense of superiority that drivers of large vehicles get when they look down on drivers of small ones. There was a spell in the 1950s and 1960s when the feature staircase slipped into the lounge as a brief conversation piece, but soon it slipped back to the hall where it belonged. The practice of placing stairs centrally in the hall has survived for three centuries. Its position was not without its critics. In a practical approach to the subject of illness, J.C. Loudon proposed that the stairs should commence in the entrance porch of the house so that 'in the case of sickness . . . the bedrooms may be communicated with without passing through the back or front

Below stairs. In most town houses built from the end of the 1700s the stairs to the basement also led to the kitchen quarters, the place of work for the serving classes.

kitchen'. And if all went horribly wrong? 'In the case of death . . . the remains may be carried down stairs while the family are in the front room.'

The staircase is the most complex and expensive piece of joinery in any house. It is an archaic structure and its component parts are described in arcane terms. There are newels and balusters, finials and risers, treads and nosing, and, exhibiting a curious preoccupation with things canine, dog gates and curtails. Newels were the upright posts set at the top, bottom and turn of the stairs, which obstructed the progress of anyone trying to slide down the handrail. Balusters were the rods that connected the handrail to the stairs, their name, obscurely, derived from the word for the wild pomegranate flower. (Since the pomegranate was a traditional symbol of welcome, a carved wooden pomegranate often appeared on the staircase, usually placed as a finial on the newel.) Risers, treads and nosings referred to the stair itself, the tread being the step, the riser the vertical face of the next step and the nosing the rounded front edge of the step. Batty Langley advised that 'the height of the steps should not be less than 5 inches, nor more than 7 inches, except in such cases where necessity obliges a further rise'. The width of the step should be not less than 10 inches 'although some allow 18 inches, which I think too much. The light to a stair-case should always be liberal.'

Dog gates were installed, like contemporary stair gates designed to prevent children falling down – or up – the stairs, to stop the house dog ascending to its master's bed chamber. The curtail referred to the lowest step where the outer edge was carried round in a scroll; its shape was said to suggest the stumpy, docked tail of a dog. Yet another canine allusion was the dog-legged stair, a staircase that lacked any central well and where the flights returned parallel to one another, each return being marked by a landing.

The antiquity of the staircase might explain one final curious feature: the appearance of ghosts. Photographs purporting to show ghosts gliding up or down the stairs include that of a shrouded figure seen climbing the Tulip staircase at the late Queen Mother's house in Greenwich, and the Brown Lady of Raynham, photographed gliding down the ancient staircase at Raynham Hall in Norfolk in 1936. The bed chamber ranks as the most haunted place in the house, but the staircase comes a close second.

Mr Shanks's Flushing Loo

An apocryphal tale circulating in the 1930s tells of an English lady approached at a soirée by an inebriated man.

'Where's the lavatory?' he asks.

'On the right of the entrance hall you will find a door with the notice GENTLEMEN written upon it,' she replies coldly. 'Disregard the warning, go right in and you will find what you want.'

The natural reticence to refer to the lavatory (or toilet, WC, bog, pleasants, loo, jakes, powder room, head or convenience) has led to a litany of euphemisms. The English used to ask to 'use the cloak room' or be shown 'the geography of the house'. The Welsh request the *ty bach* or little house. A biblical reference speaks of going to 'the place where one covers one's feet', while Shakespeare in *Timon of Athens* and *Troilus and Cressida* speaks of the 'draught' and Richard Codrington in *The Mirror of History* (1653) of the 'stool of easement'. Americans use the john and the rest room, the Danes *At ga hvor selv kongen gar alene* – the place where the king goes alone. The French, having put their troublesome monarchs to death, perversely set off to where *le roi va à pied* – where the king goes on foot.

In England in 1871 it fell to an English prince, later King Edward VII, to bring matters punningly to a head. The Prince of Wales nearly died when he caught typhoid during a stay with the Earl and Countess of Londesborough at their lodge near Scarborough. Typhoid outbreaks regularly slaughtered the poor in their thousands. On this occasion it took the lives of a fellow guest, the Earl of Chesterfield, and the prince's groom who had been staying with him. (Kilvert recorded in his diary: 'Thersie was teaching Florence and asking her who died on the Cross. Lord Chesterfield, replied Florence promptly, having heard a great deal lately about his death in connection with the Prince of Wales and Londesborough Lodge.') Poor plumbing was blamed for the outbreak.

On his recovery the prince reportedly told his aides: 'If I hadn't been born a prince, I'd have become a plumber.' It was a doubtful ambition, but the prince's interest in plumbing nevertheless prompted an investigation into sanitary arrangements at the royal households. To the astonishment of all, every sanitary device in Buckingham Palace was found to be faulty save one: the Shanks Number Four, installed in the servants' quarters and performing perfectly for everyone from the bootboy to the butler. This was, to use its proper name, Shanks's Patent Flexible Valve Closet. Listed as Number Four in Shanks's catalogue, it was a model of simplicity.

Its originator, John Shanks, was a typical Victorian industrialist. An inveterate inventor (he registered around a hundred inventions

A companionable three-seater 'crapper' restored and preserved for posterity at the Avoncroft Museum of Buildings.

at the Patent Office) and a shrewd businessman, he recognised the potentially profitable link between brass farthings and health legislation. He had already patented his Number Four flushing device in 1864 when an unwise business partnership bankrupted him. His brother Andrew was compelled to carry on the business at Barrhead, near Glasgow, until the creditors could be paid off.

Shanks was born, the son of a handloom weaver, at Paisley in Glasgow in 1826.

> How sweet to move at summer's eve
> By Clyde's meandering stream,
> When Sol in joy is seen to leave
> The earth with crimson beam;

123

wrote Andrew Park of Glasgow's famous river in his poem 'The Banks of Clyde'. But the banks of the Clyde were anything but pleasant. Riverside privies, worked on the same principle as the medieval garderobe, discharged straight on to the river bank. Sewage close to the river was piped directly into it and elsewhere sanitary arrangements were similarly basic. Privies with their wooden seats (some were companionably equipped with two or three) stood in back yards, fixed above pits that had to be emptied by the nightmen, to the distress of both residents and their neighbours given the noise and the smell. (These cesspits were a particular item of horror. In 1184 the Emperor Frederick I was making his way to the privy with several of his noblemen when the floor collapsed, depositing the court into the cesspit below. While the emperor was rescued, 'some gentlemen fell to the bottom where they perished,' reported the Revd Nathaniel Wanley in his *Wonders of the Little World* of 1678.)

Arrangements in the grander homes were provided by servants armed with chamber pots, slop buckets and close stools (a dresser or chair with the chamber pot concealed inside). In the mid-1700s Robert Adam designed a sideboard to cater for those incontinent gentlemen who remained behind with their port after the ladies had retired. Convinced (probably correctly) that significant affairs of state were settled during these lengthy drinking sessions, Adam equipped his sideboard with water urns, wine bins, knife boxes, plate-warming spirit stoves and chamber pots for the use of the diners. 'Nothing is hidden. I find that very indecent,' declared a visiting Frenchman, François de la Rochefoucauld.

However, Adam's sanitary sideboard was considered safer than the local privies and cesspools where the 'foul air' and 'miasmas' were believed to be responsible for causing typhoid and cholera. Once it was established that the real cause was sewage leaking into water supplies, public health legislators moved in. In 1848 a public health act proposed that all new houses should have 'sufficient water closets or a privy or ash pit'. Shanks, who began his working life as a journeyman plumber, had by now taken on eight workers in a bid to build up his sanitary engineering business at Barrhead near Glasgow. Fifteen years after the act came into force, he patented his most famous closet. Thanks to the health act (the English model was adopted in New York 20 years later) sales so boosted the company's fortunes that within 30 years Shanks & Co.'s workforce had expanded from just eight to over six hundred.

Shanks's Number Four was not the first water closet. The legendary King Minos of Crete used a water-flushed 'house of easement' at Knossos on Crete nearly 3,000 years ago. In the 1780s Joseph Bramah, a Yorkshire farmer's son, was already defending a patent for his own water closet. The famous Thomas Crapper, who in 1846, aged only 11, walked the 160 miles from his native Doncaster to London to find work, became another busy Victorian figure in the sanitation trade. His Marlboro, an attractive pedestal closet, was particularly admired when it was introduced in 1887.

As John Shanks laboured to perfect his own device, another hero of the water closet was emerging. A Congregational minister, the Revd Edward Johns was a Staffordshire auctioneer who was himself persuaded to buy one of the local businesses in 1867. It had been set up in the village of Armitage in 1817 by a group of potters who shipped in the best ball and china clay from Dorset, Devon and Cornwall, flint from Kent and sand from nearby Cheshire to manufacture sanitary ware. Once he had taken charge, the worthy cleric scored a hygiene hit with his sanitary ware at the Great Paris Exhibition in 1855. He promptly set off across the Atlantic to secure a foothold in the burgeoning American market.

Americans, like Europeans, relied on their privies. A two-storey privy still stands at Crested Butte, Colorado, the upper floor being pressed into service only when winter snows blocked off the lower entrance. Thomas Jefferson opted for an indoor privy at Monticello, the waste being held in a pan of wood before being hauled away by pulley. For most Americans,

Placing what the Welsh called the *ty bach*, or little house, beside the woodpile guaranteed a brimming wood box, according to champion privy-builder Lem Putt.

however, the outdoor privy reigned supreme. It remained an essential element of domestic life until the early 1900s, when Lem Putt arrived on the scene to offer useful advice on every aspect of its construction.

Lem Putt was the creation of an American, Chic Sale, who gave up his day job to take his cult character on several vaudeville tours. Putt was billed as the 'champion privy-builder of Sangamon County', and his down-to-earth wisdoms included instructions on a choice of colour for the privy: 'You need contrast – just like they use on the railroad crossin' bars – so you can see 'em in the dark. If I was you, I'd paint her a bright red with white trimmin's – just like your barn. Then she'll match up nice in the daytime, and you can spot 'er easy at night, when you ain't got much time to go scoutin' around.' His advice on the site of the privy was equally instructive: 'Put her in a straight line with the house . . . past the woodpile. I'll tell you why. Take a timid woman: if she sees any men folks around, she's too bashful to go direct out so she'll go to the woodpile, pick up the wood, go back to the house and watch her chance. On a good day you'll have the wood box filled by noon.'

A century before Putt trod the boards, visitors to a new hotel in Boston, the Tremont, were making use of one of the eight water closets installed there. The Tremont was designed by a young architect, Isaiah

Rogers, who, ten years later, was providing en-suite bathrooms and water closets to admiring guests at his Astor Hotel in New York. Americans, however, still looked to Britain to provide them with what would one day be described as the most wasteful piece of equipment ever devised. When the American manufacturers Thomas Maddock and William Leigh marketed their water closet (or WC) they felt obliged to have them inscribed: 'Best Staffordshire Earthenware made for the American market'.

Designs for the WC were becoming ever more elaborate, especially after the Revd Johns won the Golden Award for Armitage's Dolphin WC at the Great Philadelphia Exhibition of 1876. Mr Shanks countered with his own marble-topped lavatory with nickel-plated brass legs, a design which sold worldwide. Not to be left out, in 1885 Thomas William Twyford (son of Thomas Twyford) introduced the Unitas, a WC which sold so successfully in Russia that the Russians came to call the toilet the *unitaz.*

More expensive than conventional newspaper, cut into squares and hung on a nail inside the privy, toilet paper was in short supply in Europe during the Second World War.

Gilbert Smith's Klargester

Gilbert Smith was a man interested in drains. As an engineer he went about his daily business in Aylesbury, Buckinghamshire, resolving public health problems. But his heart, as he himself confessed, was in drains, especially country drains.

Most people give no thought to the processes that come into play when they flush the toilet, empty the bath or drain the sink. And why should they? Effluent from most homes is simply whisked away down a drain, away from the house and into the sewer. For many country people, however, there is no sewer. Isolated rural communities have to fend for themselves in the matter, guided by (or quietly ignoring) legislation that requires them to deal with their drainage without polluting the local surroundings. Solutions range from cess pits, which have to be emptied as soon as they are full, to modern bio systems that can filter sediments through natural materials like gravel and rushes, producing pond water clean enough for frogs to breed in.

Gilbert Smith's invention promised to revolutionise sewage disposal in country areas, but the British authorities resisted the idea.

In the years after the Second World War, however, the traditional solution was the septic tank. The tank comprised a pair of underground chambers that stored the effluent, which, in time, digested, settled and separated, rather like a compost heap, allowing clean water to drain away and leaving a solid sludge to be carted away. The system, thought Gilbert Smith, could be improved upon with one of his fibreglass onions. The material, glass-reinforced plastic, was so light that a single man could lift a tank, while the onion shape meant that it would withstand considerable loads once buried underground. It could be installed in a quarter of the time required for a conventional tank, and the tank top, looking like a sort of submarine conning tower, was so designed that, once buried up to its neck, it could be plugged directly into the house drains. Nothing could be simpler.

In the 1960s Gilbert Smith registered his patent as a Klargester, combining the words clarifying and digester and adding a Germanic K to give it a ring of clean efficiency. But he soon ran into difficulties with members of his own profession: public health officials were reluctant to approve the new technology. The first unit, although technically buried in British soil, was installed under US control at an American military base in East Anglia. Even then sales were slow. One authority claimed the tank was too lightweight, so an obliging Klargester worker had his own car lifted by crane and balanced on top of a tank to prove its strength. Then rumours ran round the building trade that the tanks were so light that they rose up out of the ground. (If the builder failed to weigh down the tank with water when it was first buried the force of the ground water could – and did – cause empty tanks to rise slowly to the surface overnight.) But as the iconic Klargester appeared on building sites across the country the word spread and sales finally took off. Gilbert Smith died suddenly in the late 1970s: a decade later sales had risen from around one a week to almost 350: the glass-fibre onion had arrived!

The porcelain wars finally came to an end in the 1960s when the two companies merged to become Armitage Shanks, and completed the prestigious commission of providing the WCs at 10 Downing Street, home of the British prime minister. But by now ecologists and eco-warriors were questioning the very concept of the all-too-convenient convenience. As Joseph Jenkins, a self-described 'humanure composting practitioner and organic gardener', put it in his how-to manual on composting human manure: 'Defecating in our drinking water is perhaps one of our culture's most curious, but least talked about, habits.' The nation's lips are still sealed on the subject.

Mr Twyford's Bath

The bath is the great relaxer at the end of a busy day, even though our naked vulnerability in the bathroom has given rise to some real, and some imagined, horrors. The final scene in director Adrian Lye's film *Fatal Attraction* (1987), when Alex Forrest (played by Glenn Close) comes to a watery end in Beth Gallagher's bath, played on the imaginations of twentieth-century cinema audiences. But so too did the celebrated stabbing of Jean Paul Marat, the French political leader, who was slain in his slipper bath in Paris by young Charlotte Corday in 1793. Marat suffered from eczema and had been taking a bath to ease his discomfort when Corday struck. The painter David's depiction of Marat decorously draped in winding sheets highlights the essential difference between these two bathing victims: Beth, so rudely interrupted by Alex Forrest, was about to relax in her bath; Marat was bathing, ill-advisedly as it turned out, for his health.

Bridging the divide between eighteenth-century and nineteenth-century bathers, between bathing to improve your health and taking a bath to wind down after a stressful day, was the great sanitary ware manufacturer, Thomas W. Twyford.

Thomas Twyford was the baron of the bath and the world's first mass manufacturer of sanitary ware.

In 1896 Thomas Twyford took a morning bath for both business and pleasure at his home, Whitmore Hall near Newcastle-under-Lyme in Staffordshire. In the closing years of the nineteenth century he could afford to recline in his new, full-size, fireclay bath and twiddle his generous moustache with some satisfaction. Not yet 50, he had managed the family's sanitary ware business well in the years since his father's sudden death in 1872. He had taken out more than a dozen patents, each a ground-breaking step forward in the fight against dirt and disease – and each a cast-iron guarantee of a lucrative return.

Twyford was more of a businessman than an innovator. According to David J. Eveleigh (*Bogs, Baths and Basins, The Story of Domestic Sanitation*): 'None of the major, lasting developments of this period can be attributed to him.' Twyford, however, knew all he needed to know about baths at a time when the rising ownership of a bath would be matched only by the meteoric rise in car ownership a century later.

When Twyford began to expand his father's business, first with a new pottery at Stoke-on-Trent in 1875 and then at Cliffe Vale, conveniently close to the Bridgewater Canal at Hanley, the tin bath ruled the day. A handy, portable domestic item, the bath would hang on the wash-house door until required on a Saturday night when, comfortably placed before the kitchen fire, it would be bathed in by one family member after another. Filled with hot water drawn off from the boiler at the side of the kitchen range, or heated in the copper at the back of the house, the tin bath's serviceability was threatened briefly by the self-heating bath, where cold water in a metal bath was heated by a coal or gas fire beneath. One such, exhibited at the Great Exhibition of 1851, was awarded a prize for its ingenuity.

Most people, however, continued to make do with the tin bath or, if necessary, the sponge bath. The philanthropist and chocolate manufacturer George Cadbury helpfully explained the alternatives: 'Take a cold bath, a sponge bath, or if you have neither, dip a towel in water and rub the body over with it, followed with a dry towel.'

People who lived in a smart town or country house and who employed a dependable supply of servants could expect to enjoy higher levels of comfort in the bathroom department. Celia Fiennes, that redoubtable traveller, probably welcomed a bath more than most of her fellow citizens, and noted such a one at Chatsworth in 1697: 'The bath is one Entire marble all white finely Veined with blew and is made smooth. It was deep enough as one's middle on the outside, and you went down steps into ye bath big enough

The tin bath was hung on the wall of the outhouse and once a week was pressed into service to bath the family.

for two people. At ye upper End are two Cocks to let in one hott, yer other Cold water to attemper it as persons please.'

Twenty years later Sir John Fellowes of Carshalton House in Surrey went to considerable trouble for his guests' comfort. First he created an artificial lake to feed a millstream. Then he set a waterwheel in the stream to pump water up to a lead-lined cistern in a high tower over the house. Finally this delivered water via a heating system to his lordship's fine sunken bath house. Given the routine levels of personal hygiene, it must have proved a useful addition: 'At court last night there was dice, dancing, crowding, sweating and stinking in abundance as usual,' Lord Harvey wrote to his friend Walpole in 1776.

A Victorian matron fears that she will fail to fit inside her new-fangled bathing device. (*Punch*)

Around this time Benjamin Franklin is said to have imported America's first bath tub when he brought his copper-lined bath from France. Almost a century later in 1842 Mr Thompson of Cincinnati had made for himself a lead-lined bath encased in mahogany, which weighed just under a ton. And yet thirty years later the 3,000 residents of Tucson, Arizona, still possessed only one bath tub between them. The lack of piped water supplies into the home – or an effective system for draining waste water out of it – prevented most households from plumbing in a bath.

By now, however, sanitation was improving. Connected to mains water in 1842 and a sewer system, designed by engineer Julius W. Adams, in 1857, New York served as a role model for towns across

America. In 1857 Liverpool's progressive city fathers, who had already installed a sewer system in the city, oversaw the construction of a mains water supply from the neighbouring Pennine hills. This gradual growth in town sanitation was paralleled by the massive expansion of Thomas Twyford's company, which between 1870 and 1900 became the world's first volume manufacturer of sanitary ware. Thomas Twyford, a man in the right place at precisely the right time, was destined to bring the bath not only to Britain, but to America, Russia, Australia and South Africa. When he opened a factory at Ratingen in Germany in 1901, he began exporting to much of Europe too. England, declared Muthesius, led all the continental countries in the development of the bathroom.

Competition in the market for baths was intense and by the 1880s householders could choose between tin baths and enamelled baths, copper baths encased in woodwork and cast-iron baths. Cast-iron baths, developed in the 1860s, could be glazed with 'porcelain enamel', a tough glaze which gave it a super-smooth finish. Cheaper models were simply painted with enamel and repainted every year or two. But although these cast-iron enamelled baths were relatively cheap they were also heavy and brittle: a clumsy workman could crack a cast-iron bath in two. The superior bath was one made of 'new Porcelain', a fireclay which was glazed to waterproof it. In the 1890s a porcelain bath still cost fifteen times as much as the common tin bath, but it kept its heat longer and did not require regular re-enamelling.

Finding the means to make so large a piece of sanitary ware as a bath had proved difficult. Francis Rufford succeeded in making the first at Stourbridge in 1850 and he received a medal from Prince Albert for his trouble. As the technology progressed, in Scotland especially, where leading sanitary ware manufacturers such as Shanks of Barrhead near Glasgow were churning out their water closets, cast-iron baths and lavatory basins, Twyford spotted a

Once the average home was connected to mains water, no house was complete without its 'bath room'. Mastering the controls of the cold and hot water, however, remained a problem. (*Punch*)

business opportunity. He travelled to Glasgow and head-hunted fireclay potters, luring them down south to his Hanley factory with promises of improved wages and better working conditions. Pneumoconiosis, caused by the inhalation of fine clay dust, was a notorious killer in the industry: Twyford promised every man an opening window beside his work bench. Before long Twyford's porcelain baths were selling by the thousands. Although the freestanding cast-iron bath would make a fashionable comeback a century later, with the advent of central heating and waterproof flooring, for now Twyford's porcelain bath was in its ascendancy. In the closing years of the nineteenth century Victorian villas were adapted to provide for a new 'bath room', conventionally placed next door to the bedroom.

In the model village at Bournville in Birmingham, however, the bath remained in the kitchen, being folded down from its own purpose-built cupboard. 'Baths are provided in the back kitchens, so that it may be possible to have a warm bath at least once a week . . . and you have the advantage of drying by the fire,' explained the ever-practical chocolate maker George Cadbury.

As for Twyford's own personal bath, the sanitary ware engineer was so proud of it that he donated it to the company museum at Alsager in Cheshire where it stands to this day, a testimony to the moment when the bath became more of a pleasure than a cure.

The Great Douche of Dr Wilson and Dr Gully

From winnowy women depicted on the sides of ancient Greek vessels, bathing beneath a pitcher of water, to scantily towelled 'ladies of Paris' experiencing the full force of a needle shower, bathing belles have featured regularly in the promotion of the shower. Initially, at least, it made little impression upon the British. Queen Isabella of Spain was reported to have showered only twice in her life, but the shower was more popular with other Europeans and Americans.

In Britain the shower was to be taken cold first thing in the morning so as to harden the constitutions of sturdy young English men and promote their health and vigour. It was still making slow progress in the average British home when in 1956 architects Alison and Peter Smithson set out their future plans for the bathroom of the 1980s at the *Daily Mail* Ideal Home Exhibition. In their Home of Tomorrow, the bath 'fills from the bottom at the required temperature and is automatically cleaned with foamless detergent'. They also incorporated a combined shower and drier unit which dispensed a choice of warm water or warm air. When the 1980s actually arrived the real must-have in the bathroom was

After endless preparation, the gentleman finally takes his shower only to be interrupted by news of a guest at the door. (*Punch*)

a power shower, in which 'shampoo is rinsed off at record speed and two or three children can be dealt with in one batch,' enthused one magazine journalist. As she pointed out: 'It's also an unbeatable way to deal with a muddy dog.'

The built-in power shower, which could deliver the body a refreshing wake-up call, had been fast developing as a therapeutic tool and a device for combating disease back in the 1800s. Following the introduction of Ewart's Improved Spray Bath which, with its ten different controls, used compressed air to deliver a spray of water into the shower, a needle shower was put on the market which directed beneficial jets of water at the rib cage, liver and kidneys. The unwary were reminded that such powerful bathroom devices were not to be taken lightly: 'It is a practice which should be resorted to only under the advice of a physician,' warned one American authority, Charles E. White, in 1914.

The first shower was patented by William Feetham in 1767 and the first shower bath in Britain by John Benham in 1830. But the power shower reached its apotheosis in the genteel spa town of Malvern in the form of the 'whisky and soda of the Water Cure, the Great Bath at Noon'. This 'direct descendant of Niagara, of which it is a youthful representative', involved taking a three-minute shower naked beneath a column of cold Malvern water falling at the rate of 52.5 gallons, or 238 litres, a minute. It was, surprisingly, marketed as a health cure.

The experience was designed to be invigorating. John Leech, a correspondent and cartoonist for *Punch* magazine, described it in 'Three Weeks In Wet Sheets', published in 1851. The shower, he wrote, 'is capable of launching down upon the body in a straight, unbroken column of water, one hogshead per minute, and with such force, the fall being more than twenty feet, that when it struck me straight on the shoulder it knocked me clean over like a ninepin'.

The great douche was set up inside specially built cottages, each constructed with a dressing-room on either side of a bathroom, built beneath a water tank in the roof. 'You descend some eight or ten feet, by a flight of steps, into a place or pit floored with open woodwork, in order that the water as it falls may run off from the feet. From the roof, two large, long pipes, one nearly two and the other about three inches in diameter, point menacingly down on you,' wrote Leech.

This power shower was the brainchild of two doctors, James Wilson and James Gully, whose dramatically successful hydropathy business had transformed this Worcestershire town. Hydropathy was as popular a cure for everyday ailments in the 1800s as homoeopathy or hypnosis today, and its beneficiaries included Alfred Lord Tennyson, Charles Darwin, Florence Nightingale and Kate Dickens, the wife of Charles Dickens. Dr James Gully brought it to Britain following his personal experience of the treatment at the Silesian Spa in Graefenburg, Germany. He searched for, and found, the Graefenburg of England when he arrived with his friend Dr James Gully at Malvern in 1842. The two men took over the Crown Hotel, renamed it Graefenburg House, and opened for business.

The Water Cure and its Great Douche had a dramatic effect on its portly, over-indulgent middle- and upper-class patrons. The sitz bath ('down go your most undignified parts into it,' explained one invalid in 1858) was especially effective in dealing with 'congested states of parts contained between the hips,' explained Dr Gully. But it was the power shower or Great Douche which represented the climax of the cure. One clergyman testified to its beneficial effects in verse:

> Hark, the bathman loudly bawling, –
> 'Stand up, t'wouldn't hurt a child';
> Still in vain for mercy calling, –
> 'Bathman please to "draw it mild",'
> Now 'tis over, rub and dress you;
> Now the nerves are in full play,
> 'Bathman, I'm all glowing – bless you,
> Can I have one every day?'

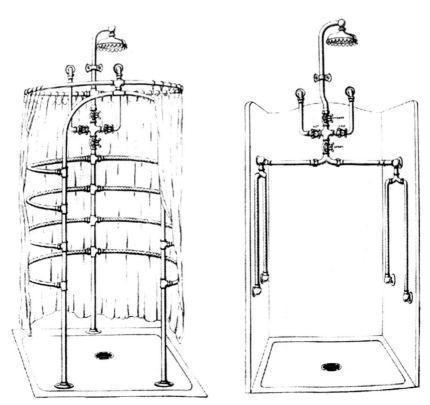

A range of 'improved, independent, needle spray showers' were put on the market in 1904 by Twyford's. The power shower had arrived.

Despite the success of hydropathy, Dr Gully and Dr Wilson eventually parted company. Gully was caught up in a scandal involving one of the most celebrated – and unsolved – murders of the day when Charles Bravo, the husband of his lover, Florence Ricardo, was poisoned. Wilson died in 1867 as he prepared to take a tepid bath. Doctors continued to offer the water cure for a while, but Malvern's power shower was finally defeated by an outbreak of typhoid fever, caused by a blocked drain, in May 1905. Writing the year before, Hermann Muthesius had recommended separating the shower from the bath (there was a trend to manufacture the shower and bath as a combined item). Then Twyford advertised a top of the range separate shower. The power shower was back and this time for pleasure, not punishment.

5

Power House

William Armstrong's Hydroelectrically Powered House

When the royal party came down from their rooms at Cragside, the Northumbrian home of armaments manufacturer William Armstrong, the manor house was ablaze with light. It was August 1884 and an army of workmen had spent the twilight hours igniting 10,000 small glass lamps and an equal number of Chinese lanterns, suspended from walls, trees and balconies.

The Prince and Princess of Wales, on a tour of northern England, were Armstrong's guests. As they strolled out on to the terrace to admire the mass of twinkling lights on the fell side, they noted a chill, still light streaming out from the hall. As a palace aide explained, this was the wonderful new electrical light that had made Cragside famous.

In a portrait painted by H.H. Emmerson in 1880, William Armstrong is pictured as a studious gentleman casting his eye over the morning paper as he relaxes by the fireside, his faithful dogs at his feet. 'East or West, Hame's Best' read the inscription over the fireplace. And, according to one biographer, Lord and Lady Armstrong led lives of 'absolute normality'. Armstrong may not have been the stereotypical shady arms dealer, but neither was he the quiet, studious type. With his flair for engineering innovation and an entrepreneurial eye on the armaments industry, Armstrong was as industrious as he was ambitious. He had also become the first person in the world to light his house with hydro-powered electricity.

The son of a Newcastle on Tyne corn merchant, Armstrong lived with his wife in comfortable affluence at Jesmond Dene not far from the River Tyne. Newcastle's Tyneside, destined to become one of the UK's giant shipbuilding yards, was still flexing its industrial muscle in the early 1800s and Armstrong was primed to contribute to its success. In 1847 he founded a manufacturing company that not only made anything from dock gates to bridges, but also some highly efficient water-powered cranes for Newcastle's dockside. His company was soon making some more lucrative items.

During the Crimean War in 1854 the British Army found itself fighting with the same weaponry it had used at the Battle of Waterloo forty years earlier. The average grouse hunter possessed more advanced, and more accurate, firepower than the average British soldier. In the 1850s Armstrong took the technology of the sporting gun and adapted it to his redesign of heavy military armaments. By 1858 he could afford to surrender the patent on one successful gun to the government and receive his title of lordship in return. When UK government contracts went cold he simply set up overseas contracts including one that involved selling arms to both sides in the American Civil War.

By 1863 he and his wife could afford to put their energies into the building of a two-storey lodge, Cragside, in the rugged countryside around Upper Coquetdale. Margaret concerned herself with the fine furnishings, ordering her wallpapers from the new firm of Morris & Co., while Armstrong dammed the local stream and installed a hydraulic ram to pump water up to storage tanks in the house.

Five years later in 1868 the Armstrongs decided to extend the house. William Armstrong, with characteristic shrewdness,

William Armstrong and his wife dine at Cragside under the pale light of an electric lamp. (*Institution of Electrical Engineers*)

commissioned a little known architect-designer, Norman Shaw, to provide a set of dessert knives and forks for Cragside. The cutlery was a small test for a large commission: the following year he asked Shaw to extend Cragside, a job that would last for the next fifteen years.

'Sir William knows right well what he is about,' wrote a grateful Shaw to his wife, a year or two before he and his partner, W. Eden Nesfield, completed another commission, Bedford Park in London. Their old English house style, a blend of the Sussex vernacular and the Victorian aspirational, would become the prototype for the pretty garden suburb and turn Shaw and Nesfield into celebrity Victorian architects.

While Shaw toiled over the mock Tudor baronial pile at Cragside, Armstrong worked on the installation of a hydroelectric generator. As dark descended one evening in 1878, a single arc light in the gallery crackled into life. 'The brook, in fact, lights the house and there is no consumption of any material in the process,' Armstrong later explained. His enthusiasm for electrical power came partly from his own fascination with hydroelectrics. Fishing a local river by a mill race one day, he had found himself musing on the inefficiency of the average mill wheel and speculating on the potential of hydraulic power. Another time, when he heard reports of local colliery men receiving electric shocks from a leaking steam boiler, he went along to investigate the possibility of harnessing this electrical power.

Armstrong was also mindful of his conversations with a friend and fellow inventor, Joseph Swan. Swan, a largely self-taught scientist, had been struggling to improve his electric light. By 1879 he had perfected a carbon filament lamp. Plugged into the power supply at Cragside, it was generally agreed to be a great improvement on the hissing arc light. 'Nothing can be better than this light for domestic use,' enthused Armstrong in a letter to *The Engineer* in 1881. 'It casts no ghastly hue on the countenance, and shows everything in its true colours.' This was no comfort to the ladies. The fashionable few who found themselves caught under its

Joseph Swan invented the world's first carbon filament lamp. His decision not to patent his idea allowed America's Thomas Edison to secure a worldwide patent for his own version. (*Institution of Electrical Engineers*)

harsh and unflattering glare still regarded electricity as a backward step in the evolution of the house.

Swan decided not to patent his filament lamp since, he felt, he owed its development to so many others. Armstrong would have agreed. As he told a commission looking into the patent laws: 'Mere conception of primary ideas is not a matter involving much labour and, it is not a thing . . . demanding a large reward.' But Swan certainly missed out on a large reward when he decided not to patent his filament lamp. In America Thomas Edison perfected his version of the incandescent lamp in 1879 and immediately registered a worldwide patent. Erroneously credited with its invention, Edison so ruthlessly prosecuted his patent that the price of lamps remained artificially high (prices were halved when the master patent finally expired in 1893).

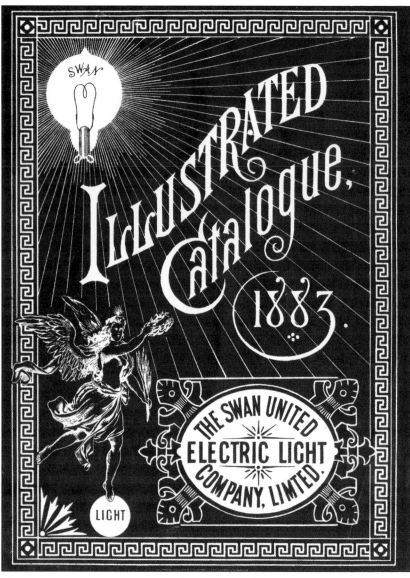

'Each single lamp . . . is equivalent to 25 candles, so that my 6 horsepower in supporting 37 lamps gives me an illuminating effect equivalent to 925 candles,' declared Armstrong. 'It is free from harsh glare and dark shadow.' (*Institution of Electrical Engineers*)

A few years later the prospect of a candle-less house had briefly lit up the horizon when Swan's and Edison's lamps were exhibited side by side at the Paris Exhibition of 1881 and at London in 1882 but further pioneering work was postponed because potential inventors feared the wrath of Edison's legal team.

Visitors to Cragside, who included the King of Siam and the Shah of Persia, were captivated, however, not only by the electric light but by other contraptions such as a water-powered lift, which carried the servants' coal from one floor to another. It was the 'palace of a modern magician', reported one commentator.

Almost seventy years after it became the world's first hydroelectrically lit house, Cragside was connected to mains electricity. Forty years later the British coal industry, which powered the supplies, had all but collapsed (Armstrong had seen it coming: 'England', he predicted in 1863, 'will cease to be a coal-producing country within two hundred years') and power companies began searching for renewable energy supplies. Hydroelectricity was, ironically, one of the favourite contenders.

The Candle-less House

In the 1880s poorer homes were still lit by the elementary rush lamp, in which a length of whittled rush burned in an oil-filled crucible. There was also the hob lamp and the cruisie, a pair of pear-shaped vessels, one fixed above the other; the upper one was filled with tallow, vegetable or fish oil (usually the latter: because this was the staple lighting oil of the poor, fish oil was exempt from a government tax levied on oil and candles). A wick made from a piece of twisted linen lay along the spout of the dish, dripping hot fat as it burned into the collecting dish below. The cruisie was generally hung as close as possible to the hearth so that the foul-smelling oil wafted away up the chimney. 'Fish-oil was derived from

Nearly every week an Inquest in London.

THE
MOLOCH
OF
PARAFFIN.

Chicago burnt down.   Hampton Court Palace twice set on Fire.

England insists on Safety Lamps for her Mines; why not on Safety Lamps for her Masses?

BY
CHARLES MARVIN.

R. ANDERSON & CO., 14, COCKSPUR STREET, LONDON.

PRICE ONE SHILLING.

The electric light also saved lives: paraffin lamps regularly caused deaths and terrible burns injuries.

the livers of shark and cod, as well as from seals and whales on rare occasions,' explained Olive Sharkey in *Common Knowledge*. 'A mixture of salt and sunshine extracted the oil from the livers, and when skimmed off it had to be bottled and well corked. It was a smelly source of light.'

Tallow candles, made from rendered animal fat, did not smell much better. They were prepared by dipping wicks in molten tallow to build up layer upon layer of fat or else by pouring the tallow over a wick suspended in a special candle mould. Frugal householders often made their own, tipping mutton tallow into 'two' or 'six' candle moulds purchased from travelling tinsmiths. Bleached beeswax and whale oil candles burned clean and clear, but they were expensive. (The first whale stocks to be depleted were a direct consequence of the need to light the home – 'in Greenland they have eleven hogshead of oyle out of the tongue of a whale,' reported Samuel Pepys in his *Diary* for 6 May 1662.)

The discovery that paraffin wax could be extracted from crude oil, refined and turned into candles caused the first lighting revolution. By the early eighteenth century the average household was dependent on imported crude oil not only for its candles – 90 per cent were now being manufactured from paraffin wax – but for fuelling their paraffin oil lamps. And Pennsylvania apparently had unlimited supplies of oil, enough to light up the world.

The arrival of gas lighting, which heralded the second lighting revolution, seemed to eclipse the idea of electric light in the home. Many considered even gas a step too far: such people included Queen Victoria herself, who preferred her Argand paraffin lamps to the hiss and glow of the gas mantle. The Swiss physicist Aimé Argand had patented his clever, flat wick lamp in France in 1784 and showed how a glass chimney, fitted around the wick, would increase the brightness of the lamp tenfold – 'No decayed beauty ought ever to expose her face to the direct rays of the Argand lamp,'

And so to bed. A candle made from Pennsylvanian paraffin wax smelled better than the old tallow candle and emitted a superior light. (*Punch*)

'How do you suppose I can do my back hair with only one candle?' demands the gentleman of the house. The brilliant shaft of electric light would resolve his problem. (*Punch*)

suggested Count Rumford, who was involved in a series of disputes over lamp lighting patents.

But the brilliant shaft of electric light that shone out from Cragside presaged the third lighting revolution. America was starting to light up its homes and streets: it was time for Britain to do the same. Brighton switched on in 1884 (it is now the town with the longest continuous electrical supply in the world) and was soon followed by townships up and down the country.

Joseph Swan was pleased. 'The days of my youth extend backwards to the dark ages, for I was born when the rushlight, the tallow dip or the solitary blaze of the hearth were the common means of indoor lighting,' he wrote to *The Electrician* in 1893. 'As a rule, the common people, wanting the inducement of indoor brightness such as we enjoy, went to bed after sunset.'

Dame Haslett's Power Struggle

In the 1930s there was no shortage of amusing stories about housewives trying to cope with the new labour-saving electrical devices: the housewife who stored shoes in the fridge rather than switch it on and risk contaminating the food; the grandmother who melted her electric kettle when she placed it on the hearth to warm; the superstitious who religiously unplugged appliances to avoid electrical leaks.

Anyone who attended Dame Caroline Haslett's society lunches in London knew better than to repeat apocryphal tales like these at table. In Miss Haslett's view electrical ignorance was not a joking matter. Convinced that electricity was the key to freeing women from domestic slavery, she strove to challenge the attitude that electricity was 'somewhat mysterious, a little alarming, something to be understood only by a few men of wide learning; a subject of little interest to the man in the street, and a completely closed book to the women in the home'.

The Slot Meter

In the mid-1800s, when an embryonic gas industry was struggling to name its parts, the fledgeling power companies relied on the services of water engineers and plumbers to install their newfangled taps, pipes and boilers. They also borrowed the everyday language of the water industry with its flows, pressures, mains and supplies. And, when the electricity companies arrived to service the home a decade or so later, they in their turn borrowed the same terminology.

But at first the power companies would supply only the better-off householders who could afford to pay. They even required home-owners to provide their own meters. By 1870 a pre-payment gas meter had been invented, but was largely ignored, since neither the gas nor the electricity industry saw any financial sense in supplying power to the *hoi polloi*. The meter men persisted, however.

Two Frenchmen, Chamon and Nicolas, set up a workshop in Paris to produce gas meters in 1881. Their Compagnie des Compteurs brought out a new water meter in 1883, and between 1890 and 1894 sales of their first electricity meter doubled. By 1901 they had patented a coin-in-the-slot, pre-payment gas meter and were developing the Duplex meter, which would find a place in virtually every French home over the next fifty years.

It was enough to convince the power companies that even the lower orders might be persuaded to pay for their power. Pre-payment meters were soon being offered to all and sundry in Britain, and by the beginning of the twentieth century the Royal Mint was forced to treble its annual production of copper coins just to meet the demand for a penny in the slot. The pre-payment meter had one disadvantage – when times got hard, the power company's customers were inclined to rob their own meters.

Haslett set out to change this state of affairs, to electrify every woman's home and 'ease the drudgery and monotony of the repetitive work which has hitherto been associated with household tasks'. As director of a curious institution, the Electrical Association for Women (EAW), she campaigned for women to embrace the new electrical world. Under her guidance, the EAW ran electricity training courses for housewives, published books and leaflets aimed at educating mothers on the benefits of electrical power in the kitchen and gave out free tea-cloths and dusters printed with encouraging messages about how electricity worked.

In 1935 Caroline Haslett achieved her ambition to open Britain's first all-electric house. The EAW show home, built at Stoke Bishop in Bristol, was designed 'for people of moderate income, who prefer to live in houses of better taste than the average villa'. The £1,000 construction price covered the cost of the electrical equipment. These included electric fires in every bedroom (they could be turned on from the bed), three electric clocks, several electric pokers, electric cigarette lighters, an electrically warmed toy cupboard in the automatically electrically lit cupboards and, thoughtfully placed by the writing recess in the living-room, a tubular heater to 'warm the kneehole of the writing desk'.

In the kitchen clothes could be boiled up in the Burco electric clothes boiler before being transferred to the Thor Electric Servant, 'which is of compact shape, and washes, wrings and irons, and has a special attachment for mixing and beating food'. As well as the electric car mat in the garage, there was an outdoor incinerator, not for household rubbish but for 'private papers', which 'can be lit by the electric poker'. And the average running costs for the power house of the 1930s? 'With a very liberal use for an average family it should not be more than £30 per annum.'

The completion of the Bristol house was a source of great satisfaction for Caroline Haslett and her pet cause. Born in 1895 into a highly religious family, she might have become a worthy, if

The first all-electric house, built in Bristol in 1935 and opened by Caroline Haslett, founder of the Electrical Association for Women. (*Institution of Electrical Engineers*)

obscure, Sunday school teacher had she not fallen under the influence of another woman with a cause, the suffragette Emily Pankhurst. 'Causes have always a formidable attraction for me,' Haslett later confided in her memoirs. In 1913 the 19-year-old Haslett left home to work in London. She dutifully enrolled as a Sunday school superintendent in north London, but sought out Pankhurst after the martyrdom of Emily Davison. An Oxford undergraduate, Davison, wearing her Women's Social and Political Union sash, had dipped under the rail at the 1913 Derby and tried to seize the reins of the king's horse. Thrown beneath the animal, she was trampled so badly that she died later in hospital.

Haslett joined the women's movement. 'What a time those early suffragette days were to a young girl! The joy of marching and carrying a banner, the frenzy of great speeches, the opposition to anything that prevented the coming of the great new world,' she

'With a very liberal use . . . it should not be more than £30,' thought Dame Haslett, estimating the average annual cost of powering the new all-electric home. (*Institution of Electrical Engineers*)

wrote later. But just as she prepared to go to prison 'and give my life for the Cause in any way she [Pankhurst] might dictate', war broke out in 1914. As part of the war effort, Haslett was dispatched to a boiler works at Annan in Scotland, where she was to become an engineer.

She enjoyed the work – but not the company. 'I did not marvel that the Scot is the leader of men wherever men are to be found,' she remarked with irony. But during her dull days in Scotland two incidents would harden Haslett's resolve to persuade every woman to demand her own all-electric home. In the first she found out for herself just how difficult domestic life was for the average country woman. Ignoring the Armistice Day celebrations of 1918, the 23-year-old rode off on her trusty bicycle (she had insisted on bringing it with her from London) in search of Thomas Carlyle's birthplace. She stopped to ask directions of a woman by the road and accepted an invitation to take tea in the woman's *butt and ben*, the traditional crofter's cottage.

'We walked across three fields, I wheeling my bicycle and listening to the old lady's talk. I was amazed to find that the family cat obeyed the command go fetch a rabbit, and when this was successfully accomplished the old lady skinned and cooked this gift of the fields.' The rabbit was skinned in an unlit kitchen and cooked on a peat fire in the hearth, in water that had to be fetched from the well up the road. Haslett, who had never encountered such primitive conditions before, mused over how even an electric light could transform the old woman's life.

The second incident involved her request to be allowed to attend college. Her manager refused. 'You stay here, my lass,' he told her. 'We can teach you all you'll require to learn. In any case, you'll soon be leaving us to get married so why worry your head about it?' Caroline Haslett did not fulfill his prediction. Although she enjoyed at least one discreet affair in later life, she never married. 'In my belief . . . I sincerely think that society would be happier, more sanely balanced and interesting, if women were given full opportunity to express and use their gifts.' Instead she pursued the cause of 'freeing women from the shackles of the past through the power of electricity'.

In 1919 Haslett moved back to London to join the Women's Engineering Society, later the EAW, and spent the next thirty-eight years campaigning for the emancipation of women through the electrification of the home. By the late 1950s her prediction that 'women and girls . . . will in the future form the largest bout of users of electricity' had proved correct – so much so that national electricity supplies were under siege. When factory workers returned home from their day shift, the power surge caused by millions of new Electrolux cookers and kettles all being turned on at once, threatened to shut down the power stations. British suppliers looked to France where different domestic routines left that nation with

Electrifying the home was the key to freeing women from the drudgery of housework, maintained the suffragette Caroline Haslett, pictured here in 1924. (*Institution of Electrical Engineers*)

surplus power at *le six o'clock* and plans were drawn up to plug Britain into the French national grid. The new cable-laying ship commissioned to connect the two countries was named, appropriately, the *Dame Caroline Haslett*.

But by now Haslett had fallen ill and she was in the process of giving up her highly social London life to oversee the construction of a small extension to her sister's home at Bungay in Norfolk where she would live out her final days. She astonished the architect by insisting that the floor of the new extension be warmed electrically (underfloor heating technology was then still in its infancy) and ignored his assertion that her plans specified far too many power sockets for such a small building. 'You can never have too many wall sockets,' Haslett assured him. When she died in 1957 her final wish – to be cremated electrically – was duly carried out. Haslett always was a woman ahead of her time.

Leo Baekeland, Otto Bayer and Miracle Plastics

A century or so ago electric light controls were shocking affairs. As latecomers to the domestic power market, electricity producers had felt compelled to replicate the designs of their competitors, the gas

160

companies. As a result electric light controls were made, like the then more familiar gas tap, to revolve rather than switch.

In the electrical switch a live wire was secured to a wooden base and protected by a brass dome, which, when turned, made the connection and switched on the light. Unfortunately the grinding action on poorly insulated wires frequently short-circuited the system, at best fusing the lights, at worst giving a shock to the person operating the switch. Matters were made worse by a shortage of expert electricians. In its infancy the fledgling electrical industry often had to rely on that other expert, the village bell hanger, to install an electrical system. Thank goodness then for Mr Baekeland's electrical insulator, Bakelite, a welcome replacement for those dangerous brass jelly-mould switch covers.

A New York immigrant, Leo Hendrik Baekeland developed the first plastics in 1907. The son of a Belgian maid and a cobbler, he left his native Ghent for America in 1889 and within ten years had made a reputed $750,000 dollars by selling a photographic process he had invented to George Eastman of the Kodak Company. The money was enough for Baekeland to re-equip his private laboratory at his home in Yonkers, New York, and concentrate on the science of polymers.

Polymers (from the Greek *polus* meaning many and *meros* meaning part) are chemical compounds with a chain-like molecular structure, each link of the chain being formed from smaller chains. Polymers, or plastics (from the Greek *plasticos*, something that can be shaped or moulded), had been first exhibited at London's Great Exhibition in 1862, when Alexander Parkes showed off his Parkesine, made by dissolving wood and fabric fibres in acid. Clearly this was a material with plenty of promise for home use.

Baekeland used to say that he chose the field of polymers in order to make money. As the father of modern plastics he certainly achieved that ambition. Whether it made him happy or not is another matter. In later life he lived as a recluse, surviving on

Underfloor Heating

In the 1950s a passing passion for heating floors by running electric cables beneath them had started to cool. Poor temperature control and even worse insulation were sabotaging the sensible idea of turning the slab of concrete that floored the home into a giant heat store and radiator. But early systems produced either scorching hot floors or tepid ones which required expensive power boosts. However, by the late twentieth century technology had caught up and underfloor heating was becoming the standard in new homes. It reduced carbon emissions and made the home a healthier place.

For one thing, underfloor heating dispensed with the potentially dangerous business of radiators. Fitting out the home with sharp metal objects filled with water heated to 80 or 85ºC was safer than having open fires, but radiators still caused accidents. Underfloor heating also repelled house mites, identified as a possible contributory cause of asthma. Radiator heating warmed the room, but left the carpeted floor cool, creating the moist conditions which harboured the house

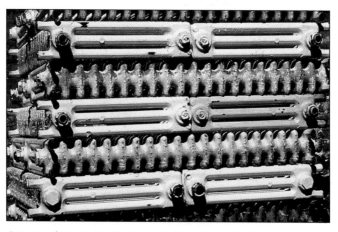

Cast-iron radiators were rendered redundant by underfloor heating.

mite. Underfloor heating created warm, dry conditions that were anathema to the bugs.

For early underfloor heating systems, we need to travel back to AD 180 at least and observe builders erecting a luxury home at Chedworth in the English Cotswolds for a local landowner. Ranging the house around a central courtyard, the builders installed bedrooms, dining-rooms, living-rooms, a bath-house, kitchen and a dry sauna beside a spring-fed plunge pool. All the rooms were fitted with hypocausts, the conventional Roman underfloor heating system: the floors were supported on tiled pillars, and the heat from furnaces warmed the pillars and the underside of the floor before escaping through chimneys in the walls. When Roman rule collapsed in Britain in the fifth century, the owner of the Chedworth villa retreated to Rome, taking with him a system of home heating that would have to wait 1,500 years before it would be adopted again.

Limestone pillars supported the floors around which furnace heat circulated. This efficient underfloor heating system was devised for a Roman villa at Chedworth in the Cotswolds more than 1,800 years ago.

tinned food until his death in a New York sanatorium in 1944. In another twist of fate, his grandson Anthony Baekeland, who spent years in a psychiatric hospital after murdering his mother, suffocated himself in 1981 with a plastic bag.

Leo Baekeland developed his plastic while searching for a synthetic substitute for shellac, a popular varnish made from the secretion of a south-east Asian beetle, the lac. Combining phenol, or carbolic acid obtained from coal tar, and formaldehyde, he produced a synthetic shellac called Novalak. It was a flop. But as more and more households were being connected to the new electricity supply companies, Baekeland continued to experiment, subjecting the chemicals to controlled temperatures and pressures. Eventually he produced a new and unpronounceable polymer: polyoxybenzyl-methylenglycolanhydride. It was a hard, black plastic that could be shaped in a mould. He called it Bakelite.

In England in the 1880s the Scottish engineer James Swinburne was working for the inventor Joseph Swan establishing electric light factories in France and America. By the turn of the century he was conducting his own experiments with phenol and formaldehyde and successfully created another plastic, which he called Damard (a word play on its texture – 'damned hard'). Only when he went to register the patent did he discover that Baekeland had beaten him to it, having patented his plastic the day before. Nevertheless Swinburne recognised a rich future ahead for any kind of electrically resistant plastic, and he set up the Damard Lacquer Company in Birmingham. Baekeland bought the company in the early 1920s and appointed Swinburne chairman of the British subsidiary of Bakelite. (The whole company was eventually sold to Union Carbide in 1939.)

Meanwhile the media was exploring this miracle material that promised to transform the home. 'It will not burn. It will not melt,' declared *Time* magazine, devoting a whole issue to Bakelite in 1924 and carrying a picture of its inventor on the front cover. 'It is used in pipe stems, fountain pens, billiard balls, telephone fixtures, castanets, radiator caps. In liquid form it is a varnish. Jellied, it is glue.' The authors went on to suggest that 'in a few years it will be embodied in every mechanical facility of modern civilisation. From the time that a man brushes his teeth in the morning with a Bakelite-handled toothbrush, until the moment he falls back upon his Bakelite bed in the evening, all that he touches, sees, uses, will be made of this material of a thousand uses.'

BIG *G.E.C.*
Radio NEWS

Expensive set performance at a popular price! That was the demand at every stage in the manufacture of the G.E.C. BC 4940 5-valve superhet. Reception is remarkably good on all wave bands. Quality of reproduction with the high-fidelity speaker is

superb. Cabinet design in mottled brown plastic is outstanding. Prices (including purchase tax) £20.8.10 (A.C.) and £21.1.7 model BC 4945 (A.C., D.C.). Ask your dealer to demonstrate it to you TODAY.

FOR BETTER LISTENING

THE GENERAL ELECTRIC CO. LTD · MAGNET HOUSE · KINGSWAY · LONDON · W.C.2

Any colour so long as it's dark. Leo Baekeland's plastic, Bakelite, had one drawback – its lack of colour.

A Bakelite bed may have ultimately defeated the manufacturers, but by the mid-1920s it would have been difficult to discover a home on either side of the Atlantic that remained untouched by what was marketed as 'the Material of a Thousand Uses'. On a typical evening twenty years after its invention the average American family would be tuned in to their Bakelite radio. While Dad read his *Time* magazine by the light of a Bakelite lamp, and his children played with their Bakelite toys, Mom, her Bakelite bracelets rattling at her wrist, prepared the Bakelite tableware for supper.

Despite repeated legal actions to protect his patent, and regular publicity stunts to promote it (such as when the Parker pen company dropped its Bakelite pencil case from the 23rd floor of a New York office – it hit the pavement unbroken), Bakelite's dominance waned because of its one inherent disadvantage: it only came in dark brown and green. Superseded around the house by coloured plastics (although in the former Soviet Union millions of householders continue to turn on their Bakelite light switches), it still had some uses at the end of the second millennium: the space probe *Jupiter* carried a Bakelite heatshield into the heavens.

Thermoplastics were a further development of Leo Baekeland's Bakelite. So called because, unlike Bakelite, they softened on being heated, they were also dubbed the miracle materials of the Second World War when they came into their own in the form of polyurethane, polystyrene, Perspex (which was widely used in aircraft production) and PVC or polyvinyl chloride. Within fifty years thermoplastics were being enthusiastically welcomed into the home for their comfort, convenience and cheapness – and steadfastly rejected by a small minority because of the environmental damage that was caused when they were made . . . and when they were thrown away.

Polyurethane was invented by Otto Bayer in Germany just before the war in 1937. Bayer, no relation to the Bayer company for whom he worked (and which would later control much of the world market in polyurethanes), succeeded in synthesising polyurethane foam in the 1930s but it took another ten years to develop commercial products from his experiments. One of its more visible manifestations is the sportsgear worn by Lycra-clad ladies working out in the gym, but it was in the walls and attics of the house that it made the most impact since one method of manufacture produced a foamed polyurethane composed of millions of closed bubbles. It proved to be the perfect insulation material.

It took a war in the Middle East to persuade the western world to start using it seriously. Although countries like Denmark and Sweden had been conserving their heat with high levels of insulation since the 1950s, their European neighbours had been squandering it. They were thus ill-prepared in 1973 when the

The plastics genius Otto Bayer demonstrates his new invention, polyurethane. It was to become the perfect home insulation material. (*Ein Unternehem der Bayer Business Services*)

Before plastics came along, early insulation was made from materials like timber, crushed into fibreboards, here being unloaded from a truck in the 1950s. (*Celotex*)

oil-producing Arab states, responding to the Yom Kippur War between Israel and Egypt, halted oil supplies to Israel's western allies, Europe and America. This was especially unfortunate for America, which, with 6 per cent of the world's population, was managing to consume 33 per cent of the world's energy. The fuel crisis passed – 'Last out, lights out: don't be fuelish' ran one campaign slogan – but it spurred on research into other sources of home energy including solar and wind power.

According to Terence McLaughlin in *A House for the Future* (1976) it was not fuel shortages but fuel wastage that was the problem. 'One of the most primitive features of modern houses is the extremely low standard of insulation, and this is the primary cause of our present energy crisis,' he declared. When the threat of global warming caused by emissions of carbon dioxide into the atmosphere turned from rumour into reality in the 1990s, researchers discovered that the average household was indeed a major culprit. Buildings were shown to be belching out 40 per cent of all carbon dioxide emissions in Europe, more than all forms of transport put together and more than the total output from industry. When it was predicted that oil production would start to slow from 2002 and decline with increasing rapidity over the next seventy years, the miracle materials of the Second World War, thermoplastics, seemed to offer

An insulation board placed in the cavity wall of a barn conversion. Increasing the insulation levels in the home can significantly reduce carbon dioxide emissions.

a solution. Polyurethane and other plastic-based insulation materials were packed in to keep the home warm.

In the world of plastics, meanwhile, invention tripped over invention. Polypropylene, for example, used in the home for everything from carpets to pipework, was separately invented nine times (legal patents were eventually awarded to two American scientists working for Phillips Petroleum in the Netherlands) and each invention made an impact on the home. In 1907 Leo Baekeland's miracle material promised to make the perfect, shockproof light switch: just under a century later, with our polypropylene furniture and plumbing parts, nylon pipes and furnishings, polyester rainwater gutters and water tanks, polyvinyl chloride (PVC) window frames and doors, and polystyrene packaging and insulation, plastics had transformed the home like no other material.

The Sunshine Homes of George Cadbury

In 2003 California proposed adding solar power to a million homes during the next decade. Germany, already spending £66 million on photovoltaic power, raised its target for solar-heated homes from 10,000 to 100,000. In Britain the government announced plans to change building laws so that every new home could receive solar power. Solar power was heralded as an energy breakthrough, a miraculous source of power which could help slow global warming and reduce heating bills. Yet as early as 1929, when the effects of the Wall Street crash were rippling out across the global pond, an early experiment in solar gain had been successfully trialled in a quiet Birmingham suburb.

Domestic solar power is no twenty-first-century newcomer. The favoured cave on the Neolithic plain was the one with a decent view and a south-facing aspect. In medieval times the word solar described the private family room of the lord and lady, located in the sunny, upper regions of the hall house. Country homes were traditionally built to make the most of a southerly aspect. But as the industrial revolution spread across Europe and rural labourers quit their south-facing cottages for the terraced slums of the city, the benefits of facing south were ignored by the terraced house builders. 'These are houses not made to live in, but to get rents for,' observed one perceptive commentator in Smethwick in 1850. And he noted 'how cleverly and adroitly they are contrived to yield to their tenants the smallest possible quantity of comfort and convenience.' (The same would be said of high-rise social housing a century later.)

Workers' homes in British cities in the early 1900s were a national disgrace. 'These are houses not made to live in, but to get rents for,' observed one commentator. (*The Bournville Trust*)

The brick back-to-backs were built on ground levelled to form a terrace (hence the name), the builders slavishly following the convention of placing the kitchen at the back and the parlour at the front. The parlour (from the French *parler*, to talk, and originally a monastic room for conversation) came to be known as the front room. Three features commonly characterised such houses: poor ventilation, inadequate heating and rising damp. The privy stood in the back yard overshadowed by adjoining buildings and hung with washing, and was often shared between several houses. And in the privy, hanging from a nail, would be yesterday's newspaper, cut into squares to serve as toilet paper.

It was here during the Wall Street crash that the average Birmingham factory worker might read about suicidal New York stockbrokers, redundant executives having to resort to shoeshine work, or Herbert Hoover's flawed assessment of the situation: 'We in America are nearer to the final triumph over poverty than ever before in the history of any land', before consigning the newspaper to the privy pit.

As the Depression began to bite into the manufacturing heart of cities like Birmingham more than three million were put out of work and thousands evicted from their homes. For a few, a very few, help and the tenancy of a solar-warmed home at Bournville in Birmingham was on the horizon, thanks to a Quaker chocolate maker. The lucky families were able to recover from the trials of the Depression in Cadbury's Sunshine Houses, tilling their vegetable gardens and reaping the rewards of an early experiment in solar gain.

The Sunshine Houses (also known as Ten Shilling houses, ten shillings being the weekly rent) were so called because they were built to make the most of their southerly aspect. The front room of the homes was placed on the south-facing side of the house; the kitchen, fitted with smaller windows, was placed on the north side. The effect of this passive solar power gave extra light and warmth and reduced coal bills.

Bournville's Sunshine Houses, just after completion in 1929. Small windows were reserved for the north-facing aspect. (*The Bournville Trust*)

The Sunshine Homes were a testament to the chocolate magnate-turned-philanthropist George Cadbury. The Cadbury family originated in England's West Country where the family name survives in at least two castles and several villages. George's father John opened a cocoa and chocolate factory in Birmingham in 1831. Chocolate then was a bitter-rich concoction believed, and later proved, to have medicinal properties (its reputation as a sexual stimulant fared less well). When John's sons Richard and George took over in 1861 the business was actually on the verge of collapse, but the brothers were astute businessmen. They turned the business around and into profit with a combination of new processes and new marketing. (In 1869 they launched the first decorated chocolate box, the progenitor of 150 years of kitsch art, with a picture of a girl with a kitten on her lap. It was painted by Richard Cadbury himself, a talented amateur artist.)

George and Richard were also exemplary employers. There were half-day holidays, cycling lessons and free material for women workers to make their own uniforms. The brothers' morning Bible readings to the workforce were reintroduced by popular demand after being briefly suspended. And when Cadburys moved to a greenfield site by the Bourn brook, which they called Bournville, they set about creating a garden city around the new factory. After the first six homes were built in 1879, close to the factory, a further 143 cottages were put up six years later at what was then a substantial cost of £150 each in order to attract 'a superior class of quiet and respectable tenant'.

George Cadbury specified even the smallest details for the Bournville homes, which he continued to build after his brother's death in 1899, drawing on the talents of a hitherto unknown Arts and Crafts architect, W. Alexander Harvey, who based his designs on the vernacular homes of nearby Warwickshire and Worcestershire. There were to be no more than seven houses to the acre, each with a garden three times its floor area, planted with six fruit trees and providing sufficient space to produce fruit and vegetables worth half a crown a week. Each house was to have three bedrooms, a sitting-room, kitchen and scullery with a bath concealed under a tabletop or hinged so that it folded back into a cupboard.

When the Bournville experiment was turned into a trust, partly so that 'the speculator will not find a footing', Cadbury made no apologies for giving his children's inheritance to the trust. 'I have come to the conclusion that my children' (he had fathered eleven in two marriages) 'will be all the better for being deprived of this money. Great wealth is not to be desired, and in my experience of life it is generally more a curse than a blessing,' wrote the man who continued to cycle the 2 miles to work and to answer all his post by return until he was well into his 70s.

Others aside from Cadbury had created model towns and villages: the Irish Quaker John Richardson built special homes for his linen mill workers at Bessbroook; Titus Salt built his workers a village and named it Saltaire after himself; and W.H. Lever played

A Birmingham family enjoys the benefits of clean air and a south-facing aspect at Bournville in the 1930s. (*The Bournville Trust*)

The Photovoltaic Cell

In the early 1950s Bell Telephone Laboratories in New Jersey set about solving an annoying problem with their communications systems. In tropical conditions the conventional dry-cell batteries powering the equipment simply ran out of power too quickly. Three scientists, Daryl Chaplin, Calvin Fuller and Gerald Pearson, undertook the challenge to find an alternative source of power.

They were working on the theories of Edmund Bequerel (who in 1839 had noted that certain materials could generate electricity after being exposed to light) and Albert Einstein (who in 1905 described the effect and won a Nobel Prize for his efforts). And in 1954 Chaplin, Fuller and Pearson revealed to the public the Bell Solar Battery, a row of boron-covered silicon strips connected in series and apparently miraculously capable of converting sunlight into electricity. The conversion rate, 6 per cent, was hopelessly inefficient. But the very existence of a free-standing, wire-less source of power seemed at the time as

Solar panels and a turf roof help to turn this house into a green machine for living in.

improbable as sky hooks. Duly impressed, a *New York Times* reporter wrote that the Solar Battery represented the beginning of a new era 'leading to the realisation of one of mankind's most cherished dreams – the harnessing of the almost limitless energy of the sun for the uses of civilisation'.

Fifty years later the PV (or photovoltaic) cell, a non-mechanical device capable of converting energy directly into electricity, was generating a billion watts of electricity, powering satellites and terrestrial communications systems and turning small homes into small power stations capable of feeding surplus energy back into the national grid. Still too expensive for everyday, domestic use, PV cells were nevertheless being used to roof homes and businesses by environmentally conscious home-owners – and prices were coming down.

The battery that had started it all was put on display at an energy conference in Japan in 2003. While its inventors, Chaplin, Fuller and Pearson, had all since died, the original Solar Battery lived on, if a little dimly: tests showed it to be still generating power.

Photovoltaic sun-seeking solar panels mounted on the roof of a self-build development in Bristol.

social engineer to his Liverpool factory workers when he built Port Sunlight. Unlike his fellow philanthropists, however, Cadbury was building his new *rus in urbe*, his gardens in the town, not for his factory force but for anyone who could afford them. And with measurable benefits: when the health of Bournville's children was compared to those in Floodgate Street, a poor part of Birmingham, the average Bournville girl was found to be 9 pounds heavier than her inner city cousin. Infant mortality rates had also been halved.

Even before the advent of its solar-warmed houses, Bournville was set to become the prototype of the garden city and, if not the prototype then certainly the forerunner of the twentieth-century suburban estate home. The idea of the garden city, where residents would live in pretty homes on tree-lined streets or clustered around a green, had been promoted by a parliamentary reporter and inventor, Ebenezer Howard. When a Garden City Association convened its first conference in 1901 Bournville was its obvious host.

Cadbury's views seem eccentric today. He issued villagers with Suggested Rules of Health, promising them: 'If you follow the rules . . . you will probably live ten years longer than those who ignore them. Never allow water to stand on tea more than three minutes, or tannic acid is developed which is injurious,' he advised, and 'furnish your sleeping apartments with single beds; double beds are now little used in civilised countries except in the United Kingdom'.

After his death the Bournville Trust continued to experiment, and not just with the Sunshine Houses which still stand today. In the 1950s and 1960s workers from local firms like Lucas and Austin formed self-build groups to construct their own homes. In the 1970s a group of low-energy homes for older people was equipped with solar-powered hot water systems. In the 1990s an entire solar village was built with large, south-facing windows, smaller north-

'Furnish your sleeping apartments with single beds: double beds are now little used in civilised countries except in the United Kingdom' was one of George Cadbury's Suggested Rules of Health. (*The Bournville Trust*)

facing windows, thermal blinds and extra insulation to reduce heat loss. Over a third of the energy was supplied by the sun. 'There is nothing of this kind in England yet carried out with the principles that I should like to adopt,' Cadbury had explained as he outlined his ideas in the 1890s. He would be pleased today that his spirit lives on.

6

House Proud

Flying Fitted Kitchens

In the early 1950s Joan Walley, head of Household Science at the Queen Elizabeth College, London University, delivered a crushing assessment of the average British kitchen. 'Today in the United Kingdom our heritage of beautiful houses from the past is outstanding, but is not matched by a legacy of fine kitchens. In this field we are indeed outstripped by Sweden, New Zealand, Australia and the United States of America.' It was, apparently, the women's fault. 'The housewife may blame the architects and builders . . . for these deficiencies, but in the long run it is all too true that she gets what she deserves.' And what she got, thought Walley, was a kitchen that was 'not as convenient as it could be'. Housewives should have paid attention to what was happening in the United States.

Fifty years earlier men in white overalls and armed with clipboards and stop-watches had arrived on the American factory floor. Their business was 'method study and work measurement', but, as their role was to calculate the time it took to complete any job and make recommendations for improvements, they were dubbed the time-and-motion men. As popular with factory owners as they were unpopular with the workers, there was no doubting their influence. It was only a matter of time before they hit that workplace of the home, the kitchen.

In 1913 Christine Frederick published *The New Housekeeping*, her own time-and-motion assessment of the home. In it she suggested that the kitchen should be as small as possible to reduce wasteful time spent moving between work surfaces. She also insisted that the kitchen should be a place where food was prepared: it was not, she reminded her readers, a dining-room or a laundry. The efficient, clean and hygienic fitted kitchen could not be far behind pronouncements like these.

Frederick's thoughts were well received in Germany. When her book was published in Berlin in 1922 it inspired the Frankfurt kitchen, specifically designed for small homes. This ship's galley of a kitchen measured a mere 3.5 × 1.9m (11.5 × 6ft) and incorporated cupboards that reached from floor to ceiling. There was even a place for the kitchen operator to sit: a fold-away stool was incorporated into the design. A year later Bauhaus architects in Weimar put up the *Haus am Horn*, a new steel and concrete home, to showcase their designs. In the kitchen, created by Marcel Breuer, function marched behind form with fitted cupboards, continuous work surfaces and a neat line of matching storage jars. The term Bauhaus (from *bauen* to build and *haus* or house) had been coined by the Modernist architect Walter Gropius. His own kitchen at Dessau, designed in 1926, was a model of efficiency with its washing machine and eye-level oven.

Within a decade the American Westinghouse Kitchen Planning Department was promising to 'design such a kitchen for your home, arranging it scientifically to save you steps and motion'. American housewives brought the language of the factory floor to their kitchens as they efficiently 'purchased supplies' and 'loaded up units'. Their British sisters, meanwhile, were still charmingly 'shopping for groceries' to be 'put away in cupboards'. Some years before Hermann Muthesius had noted this obstinate resistance to

The kitchen range takes centre stage in the unfitted kitchen of a pre-Second World War British home.

change in his *Das Englische Haus*. English kitchens, he observed, were rigidly divided into wet working areas, where the cleaning was done, and dry working areas where food was prepared. Despite the inconvenience English housewives still tended to place the cooking stove in an alcove. Were they nostalgic for the open fire and the inglenook, he wondered?

The situation was little improved by the 1940s. In an age of speed, movement and efficiency, the British kitchen was, quite frankly, a mess, 'presenting disadvantages from technical, practical and hygienic points of view', claimed the copywriter of one kitchen brochure in 1948. 'The so-called modern kitchen of the last decade has consisted of a number of appliances and furnishings obtained from a variety of manufacturers, resulting in a collection of units of various shapes, sizes and finishes, lacking in uniformity,' complained the author. Fortunately the fitted kitchen was on its way. It finally blew in to Britain in the 1940s thanks partly to the father of streamlining Norman bel Geddes, and partly to some under-employed British munitions workers.

As Europe geared up for the grizzly business of war in 1939, millions of Americans were trooping through the New York World's Fair. The talk of the Fair was the General Motors' pavilion, voted the best presentation in the show, where visitors could walk past a vision of the future, a country neatly zoned into skyscrapers, six-lane highways and fine green parkways. As they left the exhibit, each visitor received a free lapel pin reading: 'I have seen the future.'

The man who had given them this prescient glimpse was Norman bel Geddes. Born in Adrian, Michigan, in 1893, he and his younger brother had been brought up by their mother after their father lost the family money on the stockmarket and proceeded to drink himself to death. Geddes's troubled background contributed to him being thrown out of school in the ninth grade, yet he made it to the Cleveland Institute of Art and later the Chicago Art Institute. Here he developed an interest in theatre and stage lighting, encouraged

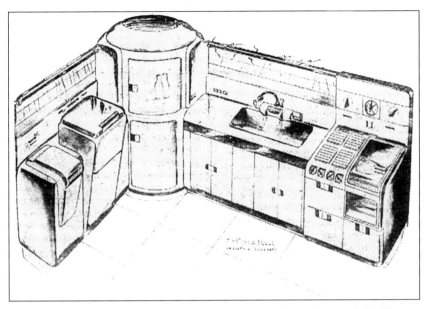

The blueprint for the fitted kitchen was a testimony to the streamlined designs of Norman bel Geddes.

by his mother. By his early 30s Geddes had established a solid reputation as a stage designer on Broadway. Then in 1927 he took a career turn and fixed his creative eye on industrial design instead. Melding the new materials of the age, glass and chrome, into distinctive, teardrop forms, he designed a series of aerodynamic wonders: a nine-storey amphibious airliner, a battleship and a flying car. None was ever built, but on a more domestic, and realistic, level were his streamlined radio cabinet, typewriter, cigarette case, furniture – and fitted kitchen units, which were included in the General Motors World's Fair presentation.

Geddes's designs inspired kitchens like the 1946 Gas Kitchen which would 'take the "irk" out of work. Everything carefully thought out to cut down on waste motion and fatigue. No more "blue Mondays".' Then there was the 1949 Kelvinator Kitchen for 'the home of your dreams'. The Modern Ranch House kitchen version promised storage cupboards beyond one's wildest dreams. They could 'hold a season's supply of staples and canned goods on one side . . . cleaning equipment, laundry essentials, even a first aid kit on the other. And there's more storage room in these wonderful counter-height cabinets and in the hanging wall cabinets with their sliding glass doors.' Kelvinator kitchens – 'whichever best expresses you' – were available in French Provincial, Early American, Cape Cod or English styles. The 'English' model was based more on sentiment than practicality since, as far as the British housewife was concerned, even a fitted cupboard was an unusual luxury in the kitchen. Change, however, was on the way.

During the late 1930s designers in Britain were streamlining a particular breed of killing machine, the fighter plane. In 1940, when no one could be certain whether Britain's interior design would shortly be more influenced by the German Third Reich or American Modernism, fighter planes won the decisive Battle of Britain in the skies above England. Pitching in alongside the sleek Spitfires and Hurricanes was the Defiant fighter, built by Boulton Paul Aircraft and powered by a Rolls-Royce Merlin engine. The all-metal streamlined Defiant sped through the air at 313mph. They did not know it at the time, but the schoolchildren who looked up from their shrapnel collections as the Defiant whizzed overhead were gazing up at their future fitted kitchens.

In 1945, as armaments and munitions factories began to explore new manufacturing markets in postwar Britain, Boulton & Paul (sister company of the aircraft manufacturer) and their competitor CSA turned to making fitted kitchens. During the war the workforce had mastered various methods of pressing, bending and welding aluminium and of cutting holes in cross-sections to keep the aircraft as light as possible. Before very long they were doing the same for the Bolton & Paul Leisure Line and the English Rose fitted kitchens. The aluminium for these streamlined cream-painted units, with their tulip-curve drawers and black handles, came from wartime stockpiles. Throughout the war loyal housewives had been persuaded to donate their aluminium to the war effort: now they were being given the chance to buy it all back, albeit transformed into a new fitted kitchen unit.

By 1953 it was possible to buy a new house for £1,700 and pay just over a third the price, £600, for a new Boulton & Paul fitted kitchen made of pressed aluminium and finished with shiny, stainless steel worktops. Later the steel would make way for plastic laminates such as Formica, Panex and Wareright, their surfaces littered with chromium-plated coffee percolators, electric toasters and food processors.

CSA's English Rose kitchen was proclaimed (by its makers) to be 'the natural progressive development of equipment for the most important room in the house'. And it was irresistible, explained the copywriters, because it was 'styled'. In 1957, as Prime Minister Harold Macmillan told the nation that 'most of our people have never had it so good', householders switched their spending from bedrooms and open plan living-rooms to fitted kitchens in ice-blue plywood and white Formica. During the 1960s parlours began to be *styled* into living spaces and kitchens were *styled* into kitchen diners. Chromcraft kitchens, for example, offered a 'stainless, porcelain enamel dinette with matching sectional buffet'. It was, claimed its manufacturers, 'a glamorous, light-hearted kitchen . . . a kitchen for dining as well as work'. Striplights, fridges, washing machines, twin ovens and extractor fans were soon added to the list of kitchen essentials and it appeared that Joan Walley's predictions ('the kitchens of tomorrow will be far in advance of those of yesterday') were about to come true. The fate of the comfortable old kitchen looked bleak.

Then kitchen designers rediscovered the country kitchen. 'Pristine and clinical fitted units are gradually giving way to individual painted dressers and shelves; microwaves are being banished to painted cupboards; and ovens, dishwashers and washing machines

There was a place for everything in the English Rose fitted kitchen manufactured by C.S.A. Industries in Warwick.

discreetly tucked away behind wooden doors,' explained one kitchen commentator in the early 1990s.

The role models for these unfitted kitchens ranged from the cavernous manor-house kitchen, where polished copper pans hung in open rows over scrubbed wooden work surfaces, to the cosily distressed farmhouse and cottage kitchen, a living-room, office and dining-room rolled into one. ('How many of us have peeped inside . . . a Welsh cottage or Devonshire farmhouse and longed to sketch its comfortable chimney corner and ample hearth?' enquired Charles Eastlake as far back as 1868.) A century of change in the kitchen had seen the emphasis move away from time, motion and hygienic efficiency towards practical informality and relaxed convenience. As the scrubbed Welsh dressers, worn wooden tables and pine plate racks trooped back into the kitchen, the future of the fully fitted kitchen was being called into question.

Keeping Time

The modern fitted kitchen can feature music systems, television sets and computers. Half a century ago even telling the time in the kitchen was a high-tech matter. 'You set the dials – at the appointed time, your electric cooker switches itself on, cooks the meal, and switches off again,' explained Joan Whitgift helpfully in the 1950s. The author of *Leave it to cook*, she was heralding the arrival of the electrically powered self-timer kitchen clock. The Hortmann Auto Time Control was a radical piece of kit: it could be fitted to an electric fire, a radio, the hall light and even the cooker. 'It is an enormous help for the housewife to be able to put the evening meal in the oven after breakfast, set the timer, and leave the kitchen until she is ready to dish up at night.'

It had taken just four centuries to get beyond having to consult the weight-driven lantern clock (so called because it resembled a ship's

The Prefab

When a housing shortage, caused by the bombing blitz of the Second World War, loomed large in Britain in 1940 the government turned to industry to resolve the crisis. The solution was the prefab, a home that could be prefabricated on the munitions factory floor before being packed off and re-erected on the bombed-out wastelands of Britain's inner cities.

Although a prefabricated Portable House made of cast iron had been built for export in the 1850s, it was the invention of a soldier and mining engineer, Lieutenant Colonel Peter Nissen, that saw thousands of prefabricated corrugated iron and timber panelled units built during the First World War.

Towards the end of the Second World War the prefab returned when the British government commissioned volume house builders like Taylor Woodrow to come up with designs for a successor to the Nissen hut. The result, an aluminium, steel and asbestos prefab bungalow, was expected to last around twenty years. Sixty years later there were plenty of tenants more than content with their little aluminium palaces.

The British wartime prefab came equipped with a bathroom, built-in cupboards – and a fitted kitchen.

The preassembled kitchen unit had hot and cold running water, a gas or electric cooker, a copper for washing and a built-in refrigerator. On the other side of the wall was what amounted to a luxury fitted bathroom with hot and cold water and a heated towel rail.

The prefab fitted kitchen did not disappear after the war. In the 1990s the Swedish company Bo Klok (pronounced 'boo cloak' and translated as 'live smart'), formed by Skanska builders and IKEA, the company that made flat-pack furniture famous, began constructing prefabricated apartments in Sweden. Made in a factory and delivered to the site in twenty flat packs, the Bo Klok house came complete with a fitted IKEA kitchen. The build costs of these twenty-first-century prefabs were based not on how cheaply they could be made but on what the average family could afford to pay for them. The *Daily Mail* heralded them as 'some of the most affordable stylish homes to come on to the market for years'.

An estate of modern prefabs in Sweden, built by Skanska and IKEA in the 1990s. The new homes were Bo Klok, 'live smart', homes.

lantern) before setting the lamb to roast. The lantern clock was gaining popularity in the late 1500s, because it needed winding only once every 24 hours, and because it sported two hands. Many earlier clocks possessed the hour hand only. But by the 1700s the average household might mark the progress of the day with the pendulum clock invented by a Dutch scientist, Christiaan Huygens, in 1656.

Soon the rhythmic tick and chimes of the long-case clock, which could run for up to eight days without winding, were regulating matters in the home. Long-case clock making was a cottage affair where each house had its workshop and each workshop made one particular movement for the clock. A local engraver would make the dial and a cabinet maker the housing. It was the apprentice's job to call round to each workshop delivering the raw materials and collecting the hand-made parts for

the finisher. After 1770 painted dials, many of them made in Birmingham, Newcastle and Halifax, started to appear. Some long-case clocks were elaborate, expensive timepieces with highly decorated veneers and marquetry, but for many the country long-case with its rustic oak cabinet and hand-painted face was an uncomfortable reminder of a family's rough country origins. By the late 1800s (and after a popular song of 1878 by Henry Work had it dubbed the grandfather clock) it was replaced in the hall by the more fashionable pendulum wall clock and by marble and porcelain confections set on the mantelpiece.

Telling the time was no problem in this Wiltshire village, where an unusual door was fitted with its own clock.

For those who could afford neither, the parish clock or the angelus bell marked the passing of time . . . except on the Aran Isles where the islanders seemed content to let time pass by without any mechanical reminders. In the early 1900s the playwright J.M. Synge went to stay on the three islands 30 miles off the coast of Galway in Ireland:

> Every article on these islands has an almost personal character, which gives this simple life, where all art is unknown, something of the artistic beauty of mediaeval life. . . . The kitchen . . . is full of beauty and distinction. The red dresses of the women who cluster round the fire on their stools give a glow of almost Eastern richness and the walls have been toned by turf-smoke to a soft brown that blends with the grey earth-colour of the floor.

The raw beauty of island life had one drawback: no one possessed a kitchen clock. Instead the islanders relied on their inner circadian rhythms and the position of the sun in the cottage doorway. Each cottage, explained Synge, had a cross-passage with a door to the outside at either end. 'If the wind is northerly the south door is opened, and the shadow of the door-post moving across the kitchen floor indicates the hour; as soon, however, as the wind changes to the south the other door is opened and the people, who never think of putting up a primitive dial, are at a loss.'

When the wind ran in from the north, the woman in whose cottage Synge was staying produced his meals at the right time. But when the wind blew from another direction 'she often makes my tea at three o'clock instead of six'. If the mistake was pointed out, the old woman would simply return Synge's tea 'to simmer for three hours in the turf'.

Assistance, in the form of the battery-powered clock, was on its way. An electric clock was invented in 1918 by one Henry Ellis

193

A 'synchronous electric clock', launched in the late 1940s, came too late for J.M. Synge on the timeless Aran Islands, where the people 'never think of putting up a primitive dial'.

Warren, and in 1928 a company set up in New York fifty years earlier by Czech immigrant Joseph Bulova introduced the first clock radio. By 1920 the highly accurate quartz crystal clock was invented and finally in 1957 the Hamilton Watch Company of Lancaster, Pennsylvania, produced a timepiece where the traditional balance-wheel mechanism was powered by a battery instead of a mainspring. There was one more development to come. In the 1968 film *2001: A Space Odyssey*, director Stanley Kubrick featured a strange-looking clock where time was displayed in red digital numerals. The digital battery clock, loaned to the film makers by Hamilton, had arrived.

The True Aga Saga

In September 1912 a 33-year-old inventor, Nils Gustaf Dalén, was experimenting with a gas accumulator at his laboratory in Sweden when it exploded. The accident destroyed part of the building and almost killed Dalén. He was still recovering when he received the Nobel Prize for physics 'for the invention of self-operating regulators which in combination with gas accumulators can be used to light lighthouses and buoys'. Sadly, he was unable to read the citation. The accident had blinded him.

Dalén, however, was a fighter. Within a year he was back at work, running his company, Aktiebolaget Gas Accumulator, with the aid of a legendary memory and the recently invented telephone. He had not been idle during his convalescence either. In his year away from work Dalén had invented a pioneering household stove. Naming it the Aga after the initial letters of his company, he also, unwittingly, helped to launch a literary genre.

Dalén had been preoccupied by the business of fuel conservation. He had applied his theories to lighthouse technology and now, blind and forced to recuperate at home, he wanted to know why the same principles could not be applied to the family stove. What was needed, he decided, was a low-energy cooker, one which would

Gustaf Dalén, blinded by an accident at his work, devoted himself to redesigning the kitchen stove during the dark days of his convalescence. (*Aga-Rayburn*)

run for a full twenty-four hours on one 3.5kg filling of coke. He reasoned that turning the cooker on and off was highly inefficient and that it would be better to store the heat in an insulated stove made of cast iron. He also decided that the stove should cook with the minimum of supervision and the maximum of economy on hot plates or in ovens that used direct radiant heat – he wanted none of the paraphernalia of gas burners or electrical elements.

Dalén had a history of clever inventions behind him. During his boyhood on the family farm at Stenstorp in Västergötland he had come up with a device that simultaneously switched on the light and made the morning coffee. Despite this, one teacher dismissed him as being 'of no use for anything'. In 1892 Gustaf took over the family farm, together with a dairy, market garden and seed merchants, and resigned himself to life as a farmer. He also adopted his mother's maiden name, Dalén, dropping his surname, Johansson. But he continued to invent and experiment, and when he devised a milk-fat tester for checking the quality of milk, he shared his idea with fellow inventor Gustaf de Laval. Laval recognised Dalén's talent and persuaded the young man to go and acquire an education. Dalén sold the farm and took a degree in technology. By the turn of the century he had qualified, married Elma Persson, started work as a designer at a Stockholm firm and founded a profitable partnership with his student friend Henrik Celsing.

From then on Dalén, who registered more than a hundred patents, followed success with success. His commercial inventions included an energy-saving method for lighting lighthouses and a sun-sensitive valve which could detect light levels and switch the light on or off accordingly. He and Celsing's company, Svenska Carbid and Acetylen, landed a £60,000 contract for a lighthouse system on the Panama Canal and when he and Celsing developed a street lighting system based on acetylene gas it was promptly bought by the township of Ängelholm. Svenska changed its name to

The Aga was a Swedish invention, but buyers in Britain needed to be reassured that it was 'British-made throughout'. (*Aga-Rayburn*)

Cut down fuel bills
with an AGA Cooker
REGD. TRADE MARK

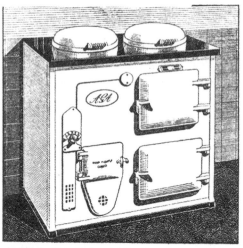

★

THE GOVERNMENT ASKS FOR FUEL ECONOMY. THE AGA COOKER PROVIDES IT

★

COMPLETE FREEDOM FROM BREAKDOWNS OR EMERGENCIES

★

Model C—Standard model for the average household Guaranteed fuel consumption less than 2 tons of coke or anthracite a year. Even the largest Aga Domestic Cooker is guaranteed to burn less than 3 tons of fuel a year.

An Aga Cooker is entirely independent and self-contained. It has the lowest fuel consumption of any cooker in the world of like capacity. It is capable of *any* kind of cooking. It keeps in night and day and can be used for cooking at night, or in the small hours of the morning, just as readily as at midday.

Write for full particulars to :
AGA HEAT LTD

1 Orchard House, 30 Orchard Street, London, W.1. Showrooms: 20 North Audley Street, London, W.1. Mayfair 6131.

The Aga Cooker is the original heat storage cooker. **IT IS BRITISH MADE THROUGHOUT.** *The word Aga is the registered trade mark of Aga Heat Limited. Proprietors : Allied Ironfounders Limited.*

Ideal after a late night on the tiles, the Aga promised to spring into action and service the needs of householders – whatever their class. (*Aga-Rayburn*)

198

the Aktiebolaget Gas Accumulator and in 1909 the farmer's boy from Västergötland became company chairman.

For the next twenty-five years Aktiebolaget Gas Accumulator would manufacture cars, aviation parts and the famous AGA-Baltic movie equipment. The stove, Dalén's last major invention, was launched in 1929, but it was considered to be an incongruous product for a company such as Aktiebolaget Gas Accumulator and in 1932 it was shipped to the UK to be made under licence there.

When Sweden stopped making the Aga, the job of constructing the castings moved to the cradle of the industrial revolution, Coalbrookdale in Shropshire. The first Aga was sold to America in 1934 and over the next sixty years Aga stoves were installed in lighthouses, narrowboats, trains, both the North and South Poles and, of course, country homes across the world. By the 1950s it was a traditional feature of the farmhouse kitchen, faded, dusty and, as often as not, shipped out and replaced when new owners moved in. However, the old Aga was valued by at least one West County farmer. At the outbreak of the Second World War, fearing that Devon would shortly be invaded by German paratroopers, the farmer removed his Aga and buried it in the farmhouse garden. When the war ended in 1945 he lifted his Aga from its earthy grave and returned it to pride of place in the kitchen.

A 1950s brochure for the Aga extolled the virtues of the stove under the title 'The Saga of the Aga'. When British novelist Joanna Trollope published her first novel in 1978, *Eliza Stanhope*, it was dubbed an Aga saga – and became the first of a literary genre of cosy, country kitchen dramas. By now the Aga, still capable of running for twenty-four hours on one filling of solid fuel, was being rebranded in new colours and converted to run on oil or gas. Sales increased, to America especially, despite the fact that in the nearly ninety years since it emerged from the blind inventor's drawing-board microwave ovens, freezers and instant meals had made the business of cooking in the kitchen unnecessary. Gustaf Dalén's Aga had become a kitchen icon.

Feng Shui

A host of potential disasters threatens the domestic harmony of the home: bringing white May blossom into a house, breaking a mirror or failing to cover one in a thunderstorm, spilling salt, opening an umbrella indoors, placing shoes on a table or allowing a glass to 'sing' (both these could result in the death of a sailor at sea), or letting knives cross on a dining table. The wise new home-owner should bear bread and salt into each room to reassure the house spirits, while an upturned horseshoe over a door should prevent evil spirits from entering the home. Burying a coin (and even an animal) in the foundations of a new home was also expected to appease any potentially malevolent spirits. For those with triskaidekaphobia, it was the number thirteen that seemed to endanger them. The Romans feared number thirteen as did the Norse people, recalling the trouble that arose when, as twelve gathered for a feast, a troublesome thirteenth spirit, Loki, entered and

Feng Shui transforms the home by balancing the core elements *yin* and *yang*, or water and wind.

immediately caused a row. Given the history of number 13, it might be better to live at no. 14.

Even avoiding these perils might not be enough to safeguard the home since the internal domestic arrangements could be blocking the householder's creativity, making them irritable, unhappy, drowsy or poor. The solution was the Eastern art of Feng Shui. For centuries its practitioners claimed to be able to reduce or eliminate energy leaks in the home, removing barriers blocking the energy flow and clearing a path through to pools of energy which could be finally released.

Feng Shui focuses on the core elements of wind and water. Wind – *yang* – is light and active; water – *yin* – passive and dark. Harmoniously combined, the two will ensure that the breath of life, the *chi*, flows satisfactorily through the home. Positioning a toilet in the wrong part of a home could rupture the proper path of *chi* and leave the occupier flushing their health away. Placing a sculpture of a horse, an animal naturally full of fire and thus a *yang* creature, in an auspicious position could compensate for a home filled with too much *yin*.

A favoured Feng Shui approach revolves around the four pillars of the home – entrances, bedrooms, stoves and desks. Entrances are especially important. That of London's Buckingham Palace is said to be particularly poor and a threat to any family living there, not only because of the absence of plants on the forecourt but because of the poisoned arrow created by Pall Mall which points threateningly at the front door.

Despite its apparently unscientific approach to creating a harmonious home, Feng Shui has been hailed (admittedly by its proponents) as one of the environmental sciences of the twenty-first century. Our preoccupation with living in homes that are attractive, healthy and sustainable, and that work well, has ensured a Western future for this Eastern philosophy.

Home Do-It-Yourself

Houseproud and handy, we have been receiving instructions on how to hang clocks, kitchen cupboards, shelves and wallpaper for well over a century. And for well over a century we have been doing it ourselves. Early home improvements were carried out in the field: the cottager swept his own chimney with a holly bough tied to a hemp rope; the farmer whitewashed his own walls. Those home repairs that lay outside the capabilities of the householder, such as mending the latch on the front door or fixing a broken casement window in the dairy, were passed on to some village artisan. The multi-tasking blacksmith, able to patch a kettle or fix a broken fireback, was a particular asset in any country community.

However, by the end of the nineteenth century largely rural populations had become largely urban ones. According to the 1851 census around half the people in England and Wales lived in rural surroundings. By 1911 just under 80 per cent had moved to towns and their new homes were not always what they promised to be. The Victorian commentator James Shirley Hibberd thundered at the tawdry quality of builders' work: 'If builders were not blockheads we should read art-lessons in the streets, instead of perpetually deploring the daily violation, in bricks and mortar, of every law which should control domestic architecture,' he fumed in 1856.

Many a city clerk, echoing their resourceful country cousins, felt compelled to undertake their own home improvements, not always successfully:

> April 27. Painted the bath red, and was delighted with the result. Sorry to say Carrie was not, in fact we had a few words about it. She said I ought to have consulted her, and she had never heard of such a thing as a bath painted red . . .

202

James Shirley Hibberd deplored the workmanship of the average Victorian builder and advocated that 'the persevering plodder in his suburban villa' go and do it himself. (*Punch*)

So wrote the fictitious Charles Pooter, anti-hero of the *Diary of a Nobody* (1892). On 29 April Pooter took a very hot bath. 'Imagine my horror on discovering my hand, as I thought, full of blood. My first thought was that I had ruptured an artery.' Then he remembered the enamel paint. 'Determined not to say a word to Carrie, but to tell Farmeson to come on Monday and paint the bath white.'

Nevertheless the trend for home improvement had caught on. And it was supposed to benefit the home improver as much as it did the home. Addressing not just the wealthy home-owner but 'the persevering plodder in his suburban villa' Hibberd pointed out 'those given to simple hobbies' in the home were 'healthy folks, healthy in mind as well as in body'. Indeed, he could not recall 'in all the sad annals of criminal history' one instance of a home improver 'who became a criminal or . . . who has been hanged'. He was addressing his observations to the man of the house, rather than the woman, for 'as Lord Bacon gives the text on this point: "Every man's proper mansion, house, and home [is] the theater of man's hospitality' and 'the comfortablest part of his own life".'

Charles Eastlake had already reminded his readers in 1868 that ladies were inclined to interfere in such masculine matters and 'we may condemn a lady's opinion on politics . . . but if we venture to question her taste . . . we are sure to offend'. And yet, as he pointed out, their opinions were so rarely their own: 'Ninety-nine out of every hundred English gentlewomen who have the credit of dressing well depend entirely upon their milliner for advice as to what they may, or what they may not, wear.'

Nevertheless, as the calendar marked a new century women were showing themselves to be perfectly capable of doing DIY. Candace Wheeler in her *Principles of Home Decoration with Practical Examples* (1903) observed that the task of improving the 'high, narrow city house, fitting them to the cultivated eyes and somewhat critical tests of modern society generally, falls to the women who represent the family'. She gave as an example 'one such, which is quite a model of a charming city home and yet was evolved from one of the worst of its kind and period'. The improvement was attributed to 'one radical change, which metamorphosed the entrance-hall from a long, narrow passage . . . to a small reception-hall seemingly enlarged by a judicious placing of the mirrors which had formerly been a part of the "fixtures" of the parlour and dining-room'.

Initially there was no necessity for the more affluent ladies and gentlemen to do much for themselves when there were workers around to do it for them. But when the First World War slaughtered a generation of glaziers, plasterers, plumbers and handymen, it worsened an already serious situation, as noted by Mrs Clarke in *The Country Home* even before the outbreak of war: 'The outcry about difficulty in obtaining servants is as loud as ever, and will be as long as the supply is unequal to the demand.' Mrs Clarke's simple solution was to train up the daughters. 'Girls may prove themselves sensible, but never do anything wonderful at school, their minds are not capable of being crammed for examinations.' Better, she thought, to keep them at home to 'undertake certain fixed duties and the mother or father undertaking to pay them adequately'.

It was a perfect time for a handyman to be offering advice. In the 1930s W.P. Matthew began offering handy home improvement tips on British radio. He would continue to do so on radio and the fledgling television until 1955. Meanwhile a tide of books, magazines and articles full of helpful tips was being directed at the handyman and handywoman. Publications like *A Household Encyclopedia* (which included instructions on how to clean no fewer than five different types of glove) offered practical advice such as: 'Wall: damp. To prevent mirrors and pictures hung on damp walls from being damaged, glue two discs of cork to the bottom inside corners of the frame.'

After the Second World War resourceful servicemen returned home with new manual skills and new ambitions for self-betterment. Newnes' *Home Management* reported on how Wembley post office engineer Robert Ward 'spent nearly four years in Japanese prison camps, where he kept himself sane by planning how he would decorate his home if and when he saw it again'. When he did he proceeded to 'add £500 to the value of his property, though his original outlay on materials is well under £100'; among other things, he built 'a dream kitchen for Mrs Ward for £30'.

Money was still tight in the aftermath of the war and home improvements were often an economic necessity. Fortunately for do-it-yourself enthusiasts there was money to be made: 'The Make-Money-At-Home-Movement has been growing side-by-side with the great national Do-It-Yourself Movement,' declared the editor of *Practical Home Money Maker* (1s 3d), promising to cater not only for

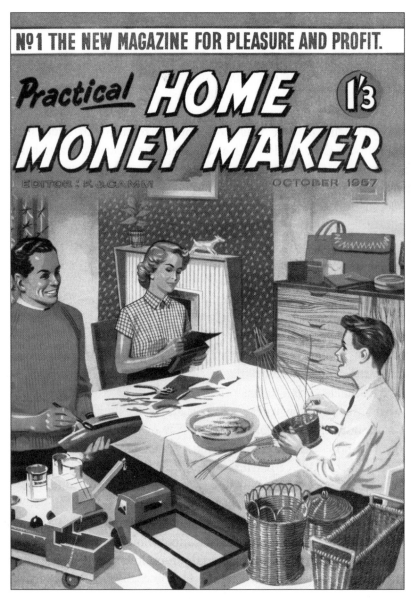

The average family would enjoy DIY and make money, promised *Practical Home Money Maker* magazine. It also seemed to suggest that teenage boys could benefit from a little lucrative basketry.

'those interested in the various homecrafts for the sheer pleasure of achievement but also for those who wish to combine profit with pleasure'. And, the magazine assured its readers, there were profits to be made from making lampshades, rugs, 'ornaments from flexible moulds' and simple glassworking. There was a regular column called 'Home Workers Chat' by L.S. Dee, who offered helpful advice and comment. No one was fooled by his by-line, but at least the advice was free. And if all else failed there was always rabbit breeding: 'Apart from its use as meat, there is a steady demand for pelts and they fetch good prices.'

When the TV handyman W.P. Matthew died in 1956, a new, authoritative figure was required to instruct the British nation on the art of home improvements. It was the turn of Britain's first home improvement hero, Barry Bucknell. No more a mere handyman, Barry Bucknell was a DIY *expert*. At the height of its popularity in 1962 Barry Bucknell's Do It Yourself programme attracted seven million viewers and a weekly postbag of 37,000 letters – the BBC had to employ ten people just to answer them. As home-ownership increased Barry Bucknell's audience wanted to find out how to conceal that ugly Victorian fireplace behind an asbestos sheet, box in those old oak beams with hardboard, and remove the partition walls to turn a dull parlour and dining-room into a thoroughly modern lounge. While the weekend brigade of 'knockers-through' pounded away with their lump hammers at Edwardian lathe and plaster walls, Barry Bucknell had to defend himself against the accusation that he was persuading a nation of home improvers to destroy their original fittings and fixtures. 'I never told anyone to modernise or tear something out just for the sake of it,' he explained. 'I always wanted things to be tasteful.'

For a while DIY remained a male domain on both sides of the Atlantic, with American wives drawing up their 'honey-do' lists and European men falling for the allure of boys' toys power tools. ('Make more money by converting your ¼" electric drill into a COMPLETE

Toys for the boys. The DIY market was driven by a demand for power tools – which have maimed and killed thousands of people.

workshop. Yours for 30s deposit.') But that cathedral to home improvement, the DIY store, was about to bridge the gender divide. One family business which had begun making and marketing wooden fireplaces in 1911 had opened a number of shops by 1954 selling paint and wallpaper. When, as Texas Homecare, it opened its first home improvement warehouse in 1972, customers flocked in.

By 1986 the local hardware store was struggling as average spending on DIY in Britain rose to £4,000 a year with double-glazing, fitted kitchens, new bathrooms and central heating at the top of people's home improvement wish list. In America, where adding a garage with a breezeway, and dormer windows to create attic bedrooms, were the hot favourites, home improvements and repairs increased by 115 per cent between 1982 and 1992. Later, as laminate floors and garden improvements took over at the top of the list, DIY became as aspirational as it was practical. However, DIY had its downside. It could be dangerous. Emergency hospital units grew significantly busier during national holidays as DIY's most hazardous tools – ladders, power drills, circular saws, chainsaws and electrical equipment – took their toll. Australian researchers attributed the majority of nearly 300 domestic deaths between 1989 and 1992 to home improvers and house repairers; Britain's Department of Trade and Industry estimated that 250,000 people were injured and 70 killed in DIY accidents every year; while the American Home Safety Council estimated that home improvers accounted for up to 20 million medical visits.

Despite bookshelves and magazine racks and television channels devoted to DIY, disasters were inevitable. British estate agents estimated that a bodged DIY job could knock anything up to 5 per cent off the value of a house. DIY dads burned down their homes and DIY mums flooded them. One west London DIY enthusiast finished off the driveway to his garage with three neat steps, insurmountable by his car; another returned from a weekend away to find that his ancient thatched cottage had collapsed like a house

Handy Hints

HANDY HINT NUMBER 1. Hanging wallpaper. Amateurs will find their task a much easier one if they apply the paste to the wall instead of the paper, which is apt to tear and give trouble.

(*A Household Encyclopedia*)

HANDY HINT NUMBER 2. Marble, to remove smoke stains. Make a paste of equal parts of whiting, washing soda and chalk. Rub it well into the stained places and allow to dry. Afterwards wash over with cold water.

(*A Household Encyclopedia*)

HANDY HINT NUMBER 3. Glass: to cut or break. File a notch on the edge of the glass at the place it is desired to start the break. Then to the notch apply a red-hot iron and slowly draw it in the required direction. A crack will follow the iron.

(*A Household Encyclopedia*)

HANDY HINT NUMBER 4. Panelled doors may be converted into modern flush or single panel doors by facing them with a suitable type of fibreboard.

(*Newnes' Home Management*)

HANDY HINT NUMBER 5. To prevent heat loss and reduce heating bills, insulate the loft. Always use proper insulating materials: newspapers and old rags attract insects and are a fire risk.

(*Newnes' Home Management*)

of cards. 'All I did was remove some non-structural partitions,' groaned the owner. Where once the DIY dad seemed to pose a threat to the professional handyman, now, it seemed, he was creating work for them.

Franklin's Safety Rods

There is no truth in the expression 'safe as houses' since around 4,000 people are killed in their homes each year in Britain. In America in 2002 there was a fatality in the home every sixteen minutes. As the novelist E.M. Forster put it: 'We are none of us safe. We are children, playing or quarrelling on the line.'

Even the home is under siege. Although central heating has defeated the Death Watch beetle (bombing and heavy artillery in the Second World War shook homes to their foundations, loosening joints and creating the perfect, damp conditions for the beetle to thrive in), woodworm and termites still feast on houses. (Termites have turned up as far north in Europe as Barnstaple in Devon, while the larvae of the Longhorn beetle, brought home by troops returning from the First World War, have mysteriously maintained a stronghold in Camberley in Surrey.) Some products designed to protect the home against them – DDT, lead paint, creosote or American tar – have turned out to be as dangerous as asbestos, once used as an all-purpose building material. Now researchers are looking into the potential dangers of volatile organic compounds (VOCs), a range of chemicals found in modern materials and often described as the smell of new things.

One of the most visible threats to the home, however, is lightning. The Emperor Tiberius nervously reached for a crown of laurels during a thunderstorm and, since the laurel was supposed to give immunity from lightning strikes, would wear it upon his head until the storm had passed. For the unfortunate Revd Graham, the vicar of Southborough near Tunbridge Wells in 1903, there was no such protection. The local newspaper reported:

> A few minutes before 4 o'clock there was a flash followed by a terrific explosion, and the side of the building was torn open from the roof. Great lumps of brickwork were flung 50 yards and more, and every room connected with that particular chimney was greatly damaged. Happily no occupant was injured, but both the vicar and Mrs Graham, as well as the servant, had a narrow escape from death.

The incident was a timely reminder, according to John F. Davie in *Country Home* magazine, that lightning could strike anywhere. 'Investigation shows that comparatively low buildings are subject to severe damage as the highest ones; indeed, for every tall structure such as a church spire or chimney shaft, that is struck by lightning, about half a dozen low ones, ranging from mere cottages and villas to mansions, suffer in like manner.'

Down the centuries householders endeavoured to protect their property in all kinds of ways. A farming family who occupied the 500-year-old farmhouse at Stangend, Danby (now removed to the Ryedale Folk Museum), preserved a 'witch post' in the entrance passage to keep such evils as lightning at bay. The post, carved with a St Andrew's cross, was well known in north-east Yorkshire for its reliability. While Jewish people could expect some protection from the little mezuzahs fixed to the door post of the home, each containing a prayer or text from the Torah, a specific protection against lightning, said to be especially popular in the Forest of Dean, was the house leek (*Sempervivum tectorum*) which was almost guaranteed to keep lightning away from thatched roofs.

Being caught in a thunderstorm was a frightening experience for householders. In eighteenth-century Europe villagers would run to the church and ring the bells to disperse the lightning. Since the church tower was usually the highest building in the parish, and the metal bells conducted the electrical discharge of lightning all too well, the results were often fatal. An investigation into the problem, published in Munich in 1784, estimated that 386 church towers had been struck causing the deaths of 103 bell-ringers during a thirty-three year period. However, a solution was on its way. The 100m tall campanile of St Mark's in Venice had been damaged or destroyed by lightning no fewer than nine times when Mr Benjamin Franklin, in 1766, proposed installing there one of his inventions, the Franklin rod. The church authorities agreed and the campanile has been safe ever since.

Franklin, who unravelled the mysteries of the Gulf Stream and invented bifocal glasses and an efficient household stove, was known as the patron saint of common sense. His lightning rods, however, would prove to be a lifesaver. The tenth son of a pious Boston couple, Josiah Franklin from Ecton, Northamptonshire, and his second wife Abiah, Benjamin Franklin was apprenticed to his printer brother as soon as he was old enough to go to work. But in 1723, pretending that he had got a local girl pregnant, Franklin slipped away to Philadelphia, arriving there with a single Dutch dollar to his name. He was 17. By the age of 42 he could afford to retire from the profitable printing business he had set up and devote himself to becoming a public servant, diplomat, vegetarian, scientist, co-author of the American constitution and America's most popular founding father.

Two years earlier in 1746 in Philadelphia he had attended a demonstration of 'electrical apparatus' by Dr Spence from Scotland. Franklin's curiosity about electricity, and lightning in particular, was aroused and he set out to prove that lightning was an electrical discharge. 'In September 1752 I erected an Iron Rod to draw the Lightning down into my House, in order to make some Experiments on it, with two Bells to give Notice when the Rod should be

Benjamin Franklin, the patron saint of common sense and inventor of the lightning rod.

electrified. A contrivance obvious to every Electrician,' he explained in a letter to a friend.

His solution to lightning strikes was to fix a metal rod to the tallest point of a building, connected to a metal strip which reached down to the ground. The rod would then attract the charge and conduct it safely into the ground, and thus earth it, thereby avoiding damage to other parts of the building.

Franklin's theories were first put to the test in Europe at Marly-la-Ville on 10 May 1752 when a tall iron rod was shown to produce sparks during a thunderstorm. The Marly experiment was repeated across Europe with Franklin famously flying a kite in the eye of the storm and creating sparks from the damp hemp kite line. The experiment might have killed him. But home-owners needed no more reassurance of the efficiency of Franklin's invention than the continuing safety of the campanile at St Mark's in Venice and a dramatic occasion on 18 April 1777 when a crowd at Sienna in Italy witnessed a lightning strike on their city hall tower. Previously damaged by lightning, this time the tower, protected by its Franklin rods, survived unscathed.

The experience was enough to convince most householders that the Franklin rod was more effective than witchposts, house leeks and even laurel crowns. As John F. Davie reminded his readers: 'If our residence is to be quite safe it behoves us to give the system of protection from lightning as much attention as we should to the sanitary system or the other arrangements for our comfort and well-being.'

In a curious footnote, however, the Royal Navy, adamant that no good ideas could come out of the rebellious American colonies, steadfastly refused to place Franklin rods on their ships despite losing an estimated 200 ships during the Napoleonic wars to lightning strikes. They finally relented in the 1830s, by which time every home of any substance had already been equipped with one of Mr Franklin's rods.

The Safe House

In 2000, researchers at Brunel University in Middlesex gave a new twist to the idea of the safe house when they invented a home that could talk to, and take care of, its own occupants. Designed by Professor Heinz Wolff, the Millennium House was like any other home except for its electronic sensors and clever computer.

The sensors, capable of detecting human pressure (or the lack of it), were placed in key locations around the home: on bath taps, door handles, beds, cooker switches and even lavatory seats. The sensors were then linked to a computer, which was programmed to detect and register the ordinary, day-to-day activities of the person who lived in the house.

If an unusual situation arose – a window was broken, the bed remained unoccupied or the occupant stayed in the lavatory for too long – the computer would activate a voice machine, which would call out: 'Are you OK?' If it received no answer, the computer would alert help from outside. If the lights went out because of a power failure, the computer would reassure the householder: 'The power has gone off. Stay sitting down and I'll call someone to come and help.' The computer could even be linked to a high-tech toilet capable of analysing the contents of the bowl and programmed to detect the early signs of someone falling ill.

Professor Wolff, famous for popularising scientific ideas on television, estimated that such a system could be retrospectively incorporated into any home. But, pointing out that most major technical innovations had taken a generation to be embraced (video-recorders were available in 1948 and email in the early 1970s), Wolff predicted that the safe house was unlikely to arrive until some time around 2020.

The Final Nail

The role of the humble nail, that piece of oversized wire sold so cheaply it can be bought by weight rather than by number, takes first place in this book's title and last place in its contents. It serves to illustrate what this history of the home has so often demonstrated: that even the humblest of items has a tale to tell.

For 150 years the humble household nail was the product of sweated labour.

> Oh, the slaves abroad in the sugar canes,
> Find plenty to help and pity their pains,
> But the slaves at home in the mine and the fire,
> Have plenty to pity but none to admire,

ran the words of one striking nail-maker's song.

William Hutton takes up the story in 1741, passing through the town of Walsall on his way to Birmingham. He was surprised to note 'a prodigious number of blacksmith shops upon the road and could not conceive how a country, though populous, could support so many people of the same occupation'. He was even more surprised when he glanced inside the shops: 'I observed one or more females, stript of their upper garments and not overcharged with the lower, wielding the hammer with all the grace of their sex.' He enquired whether these half-naked labouring women shod horses. He was answered with a smile: 'They are nailers.'

In medieval times every house nail was forged by hand. Consequently these square-sectioned nails with their L-shaped heads were expensive and the carpenters who built houses, whether they were oak-framed houses in Normandy, log lodges in Norway or timber cabins in New England, learned to work the wood without

The timber homestead could be built without a single nail being used.

the aid of a single nail, linking the beams with mortice joints and timber pegs instead.

By the eighteenth century, however, the nail had become the adhesive of the house, used to fix floorboards, shingles, door panels, wainscots and just about any other task that could be conceived. Even the arrival of the wood screw (George Nettlefield began producing screws at his Birmingham factory in the 1840s) did not entirely usurp the nail and some builders in the English West Midlands still refer to a hammer as a Brummie screwdriver.

The source of the cheap nails was the sweatshops of the industrial Midlands where women and children laboured with hammer and anvil to turn out cut nails. Cut nails were produced from sheets of iron slit into long, square sections in slitting mills and then delivered to the nailers to be forged into nails. By 1811

218

'His manhood is ashamed who sees these poor female beings swinging their heavy hammers.' One of the last women chain- and nail-menders from Cradley. (*Avoncraft Museum of Historic Buildings*)

powerful guillotines had been introduced to machine cut the nail, but so long as these Midlanders were prepared to slave away at the anvil, hand-cut nails had a ready market.

'No part of this work is work for women, and his manhood is ashamed who sees these poor female beings swinging their heavy hammers or working the treadles of the Oliver,' declared Robert Sherand in *Pearson's Magazine* in 1896. (The Oliver, named after the heavy-handed Oliver Cromwell, was the treadle hammer.) 'There are here factories where meagre little girls and boys . . . are put to tasks during their apprenticeship, against which a man would revolt,' he wrote, giving as an example a girl apprenticed to a chain maker.

'She was fourteen by the Factory Act: by paternity she was ten, I never saw such little arms, and her hands were made to cradle dolls. She was making links for chain harrows, and as she worked the heavy Oliver she sang a song. And I also saw her owner approach with a clenched fist and heard him say: "I'll give you 'some golden hair was hanging down her back'! Why don't you get on with your work!"'

At the turn of the twentieth century foggers or sweaters still ran gangs of up to 1,500 workers, turning out nails and chains in the sweatshops of Walsall, Bromsgrove and Cradley. 'The fogger flourishes in Cradley, no less than in Bromsgrove, with this difference that in Cradley it is most often a woman who assumes the functions of a sweater,' wrote Sherand, whose exposé of the 'White Slaves of England' helped finally bring the trade to an end.

Further Reading

GENERAL

Ayres, James, *The Shell Book of the Home in Britain* (London, Faber & Faber, 1981)

Clifton-Taylor, Alec, *The Pattern of English Building* (London, Faber & Faber, 1962)

Fermor-Hesketh, Robert, *Architecture of the British Empire* (London, Weidenfeld & Nicolson, 1968)

Gardiner, Stephen, *Evolution of the House* (London, Constable, 1975)

The House Book (London, Phaidon, 2001)

Jenner, Michael, *The Architectural Heritage of Britain and Ireland* (London, Michael Joseph, 1993)

Lambton, Lucinda, *Vanishing Victoriana* (London, Phaidon, 1976)

Palladio Londinensis (2nd edn, London, 1738)

Penoyre, John and Penoyre, Jane, *Houses in the Landscape* (London, Faber & Faber, 1978)

Prizeman, John, *Your House – the Outside View* (London, Quiller Press, 1982)

Reid, Richard, *The Shell Book of Cottages* (London, Michael Joseph, 1977)

Rivers, T., Cruickshank, D., Darley, G. and Pawley, M., *The Name of the Room* (London, BBC Books, 1992)

Saron, Juta, *Vernacular Architecture at the Estonia Open-Air Museum* (Tallinn, Huma, 1997)

Yarwood, Doreen, *English Interiors* (Guildford, Lutterworth Press, 1983)

INTRODUCTION

Eastlake, Charles, *Hints on Household Taste*, 3rd edn, revised (London, Spottiswoode & Co., 1872)

Hutton, William, *History of Birmingham* (1783)

Wheeler, Candace, *Principles of Home Decoration with Practical Examples* (New York, Doubleday, Page & Co., 1903)

221

1. OPEN HOUSE

Dickens, Charles, *The Uncommercial Traveller* (London, William Clowes, 1887)

Francis Kilvert's Diary, 1870–1879: An Illustrated Selection (London, Century Hutchinson, 1986)

Haddonstone Ltd, Northampton, pamphlet written by Pricot in 1770

Kelly, Alison, *Mrs Coade's Stone* (Upton-upon-Severn, The Self Publishing Association Ltd in conjunction with the Georgian Group, 1990)

Laws, Bill, *The Perfect Country Cottage* (London, Conran Octopus, 1993)

McLaughlin, Jack, *Jefferson and Monticello: Biography of a Builder* (New York, Holt, 1988)

Smith, Margaret Baynard, *President's House Forty Years Ago* (1841)

Walker, Henry, *The Country Home* (London, Constable, 1908)

2. HOUSE STYLE

Adam, R., *Works in Architecture of Robert and James Adam, Esquires* (London, 1773–1822)

Barnes, Alison (ed.), *Home Management*, vol. 2 (London, George Newnes, 1957)

Chevalier, Tracy, *Girl with a Pearl Earring* (London, HarperCollins, 1999)

Heathcote, David, *Sixties Style* (Enfield, Middlesex University Press, 2004)

Hibberd, Shirley, *Rustic Adornments for Homes of Taste* (London, 1856; repr. London, Century in association with the National Trust, 1987)

Hoskins, Lesley (ed.), *The Papered Wall* (London, Thames & Hudson, 1994)

Laws, Bill, *Artists' Gardens* (London, Ward Lock, 1999)

Loudon, J.C., *An Encyclopaedia of Cottage, Farm and Villa Architecture* (London, Longman, 1836)

Massey, Anne, *Interior Design of the 20th Century* (London, Thames & Hudson, 1990)

Middleton, G.A.T., *Building Materials* (London, Batsford, 1915)

Muthesius, Hermann, *Das Englische Haus* (Berlin, Wasmuth, 1904)

Osborne, A.L., *A Dictionary of English Domestic Architecture* (London, Country Life, 1954)

Pugin, A.W.N., *Contrasts: AND The True Principles of Pointed or Christian Architecture* (London, Spire Books, 2003)

Victorian Society, *Decorative Tiles*, pamphlet no. two (London, 1992)

Wheeler, Candace, *Principles of Home Decoration with Practical Examples* (New York, Doubleday, Page & Co., 1903)

Wilson, Michael, *The English Country House and its Furnishings* (London, Batsford, 1977)

3. HOUSEHOLD ESSENTIALS

Bax, B. Anthony, *The English Parsonage* (London, John Murray, 1964)

Britton, John, *Beauties of Wiltshire* (Salisbury, 1801–25)

Brown, G.I., *Scientist, Statesman, Soldier, Spy: Count Rumford: The Extraordinary Life of a Scientific Genius* (Stroud, Sutton Publishing, 1999)

Conran, Terence, *The Essential House Book* (London, Conran Octopus, 1994)

Dickens, Charles, *The Pickwick Papers* (London, The Educational Book Co., 1910)

Fiennes, C., *Through England on a Side Saddle in the Time of William and Mary: The Diary of Celia Fiennes*, ed. Mrs Griffiths (Field & Tuer, 1888)

Francis Kilvert's Diary, 1870–1879: An Illustrated Selection (London, Century Hutchinson, 1986)

Hammersley, Howard and Hunt, David, *A History of Richard Baxendale and Sons* (Preston, Baxi Partnership, 1997)

Laws, Bill, *Traditional Houses of Rural Spain* (London, Collins & Brown, 1995)

Warner, Dr Jill, *Allergic Diseases and the Indoor Environment* (University of Southampton, 2003)

Wilton Carpet Factory (Wessex Books, 1998)

Woodward, Christopher, *Windows* (The Building of Bath Museum and Bath City Council, 1994)

4. HOUSE WORKS

Barker, T.G., *An Age of Glass* (London, Boxtree, 1994)

Carter, Ella (ed.), *Seaside Houses and Bungalows* (London, Country Life, 1937)

Eveleigh, David J., *Bogs, Baths & Basins: The Story of Domestic Sanitation* (Stroud, Sutton Publishing, 2002)

Fiennes, C., *Through England on a Side Saddle in the Time of William and Mary: The Diary of Celia Fiennes*, ed. Mrs Griffiths (Field & Tuer, 1888)

Harcup, John Winsor, *The Malvern Water Cure* (Lavern, Winsor Fox Photos, 1992)

Jenkins, Joseph, *The Humanure Handbook: A Guide to Composting Human Manure*, 2nd edn (Jenkins Publishing, 1999)

Jirinca, Eva, *Staircases* (London, Laurence King Publishing, 2001)

Loudon, J.C., *An Encyclopaedia of Cottage, Farm and Villa Architecture* (London, 1836)

Pudney, John, *The Smallest Room* (London, Michael Joseph, 1954)

Rochefoucauld, François de la, *A Frenchman's Year in Suffolk, 1784*, translated Norman Scarfe (Woodbridge, Suffolk, Boydell & Brewer, Suffolk Records Society, 2001)

Woodward, Christopher, *Windows* (The Building of Bath Museum and Bath City Council, 1994)

5. POWER HOUSE

Barnsby, George J., *Social Conditions in the Black Country, 1800–1900* (Wolverhampton, Integrated Publishing Services, 1980)

Cragside (London, The National Trust, 1992)

Dillon, Maureen, *Artificial Sunshine: A Social History of Domestic Lighting* (London, National Trust, 2002)

Electricity Handbook for Women (London, English University Press, 1934)

Henslowe, Philip, *Ninety Years On: An Account of the Bournville Village Trust* (Birmingham, Bournville Village Trust, 1991)

Hilman, Judy, *The Bournville Hallmark* (Studley, Brewin Books, 1994)

McKenzie, Peter, *The Life and Times of Sir William Armstrong of Cragside* (Newcastle, Longhirst, 1983)

McLaughlin, Terence, *A House for the Future* (London, TV Times, 1976)

Oxford, Margot, Countess of Oxford and Asquith (ed.), *Myself when Young by Famous Women of Today* (London, Miller, 1938)

Pepys, Samuel, *Diary of Samuel Pepys* (London, J.M. Dent, 1906)

Sharkey, Olive, *Common Knowledge* (Dublin, O'Brien Press, 1985)

6. HOUSE PROUD

Davie, John F., *The Country Home* (London, Constable, 1908)

Eastlake, Charles, *Hints on Household Taste*, 3rd edn (London, Spottiswoode & Co., 1872)

Further Reading

Forster, E.M., *The Longest Journey* (London, Penguin Classics, 2001)

Frederick, Christine, *The New Housekeeping* (New York, Doubleday, 1926)

Grey, Johnny, *The Art of Kitchen Design* (London, Cassell, 1994)

Grossmith, George and Grossmith, Weedon, *Diary of a Nobody* (London, Penguin Classics, 1999)

James, Tim, *The Story of a Kitchen Classic* (Bath, Absolute Press, 2002)

Labaree, Leonard W. (ed.), *The Papers of Benjamin Franklin* (New Haven, Yale University Press, 1962)

Mabey, Richard, *Flora Britannica* (London, Sinclair-Stevenson, 1996)

Muthesius, Hermann, *Das Englische Haus* (Berlin, Wasmuth, 1904)

Steer, W.H. (ed.), *A Household Encyclopedia* (London, Spring Books, n.d.)

Synge, J.M., *The Aran Islands* (Dolmen Press, Dublin, 1907)

Uman, M.A. and Rakov, V.A., 'A Critical Review of Non-Conventional Approaches to Lightning Protection, 1809–1820', *Bulletin American Meteorological Society*, 83 (2002), 1809–20

Walley, Joan, *Home Management*, vol. 2, ed. Alison Barnes (London, George Newnes, 1957)

Whitgift, Joan, *Home Management*, vol. 1, ed. Alison Barnes (London, George Newnes, 1957)

Index

Aalto, Alvar, 34
Adam, James, 45, 222
Adam, Robert, 26, 124, 46
Adam brothers, 24, 44–50,
    47, 48, 50
Adam style, 44–50
Adams, Julius W., 134
Africa, 40, 57, 135, 110
Aga, 195–9, 197, 198
Aga saga, 195, 199
all-electric house, 156, 157,
    158
allergies, 86
Allingham, Helen, 65–8
Alps, 69
America, 31, 48, 71, 72,
    79, 81, 83, 88, 91, 96,
    98, 108, 109, 115,
    134, 135, 146, 154,
    161, 164, 168, 172,
    199
American Institute of
    Architects Foundation,
    26
Americans, 94, 102, 109,
    115, 122, 125, 126,
    127, 129, 137, 139,
    144, 165, 169, 181,
    182, 184, 186, 207,
    211, 213, 215
Anaglypta, 58
Aran Isles, 193
architrave, 37
Argand, 151

Argand, Aimé, 151
Arizona, 134
Armitage Shanks, 130
Armstrong, William,
    143–60
Arts and Crafts, 43, 49, 52,
    54, 65, 174
Ashbee, C.R., 65
Aspdin, Joseph, 5, 72–9, 76
Aspdin, William, 76
Associated Artists, 49
asthma, 86
astragal, 37, 112
Australia, 110, 135, 181
Australian, 42, 44
Avoncroft Museum of
    Buildings, 123
Axminster, 83
Aylesbury, 128
azulejos, 57

Babcock, George, 96
Baekeland, Leo, 160–9
Bakelite, 161–6, 165
balusters, 20, 118, 120
Bank of England, 24
bargeboards, 33
barn, 28
bath, 20, 93, 130–7, 134,
    136
  cast-iron, 135
  porcelain, 135
  sponge, 132
  tin, 132, 133

Bauhaus, 182
Bavaria, 10, 88
Baxendale, Thomas, 98
Baxi Bermuda, 98, 102
Bayer, Otto, 160, 167
Becket, George E., 11
Beddington lock, 15
Bedford Park, 146
Bedford Square, 24
bedroom, 15, 43, 55, 72,
    98, 119, 136, 156,
    163, 174, 187, 191,
    201, 209
Bel Geddes, Norman, 184,
    185, 185
Belgium, 52
Bell, Alexander Graham, 11
Bengal, 41
Bessbrook, 174
Biglow, Erasmus, 83
Bilston, 18
Birchington, 43
Birmingham School of
    Design, 66
Birmingham, 106, 107,
    137, 164, 170, 173,
    172, 178, 192, 208,
    217, 218
black house, 40, 41, 87
Blaize Hamlet, 67, 68
Blakely, William, 91
boiler, 91–102, 94, 99
Bolton-le-Moors, 27
Boston, 55, 72, 126

Boulton and Paul, 186
Boulton Paul Aircraft, 186
Bournville, 137, 172–80,
    173, *175*, 178
Bracciolini, 40
Brahmah, Joseph, 6, 19, 18,
    125
breezeway, 32, 209
Breton, 32, 70, *70*
Breuer, Marcel, 182
brick, 1, 23, 41, 67, 71, 73,
    76, 77, 78, 111, 129,
    172, 202
Bridgwater, 71
Briggs, Robert Alexander, 44
Brighton, 154
Bristol, 61, 67, 156, *157*
broadsheet glass, 104
Bromsgrove, 220
Brunel, Isambard Kingdom,
    76
Buckingham, Duke of, 104
Buckingham Palace, 24, 26,
    122, 201
Bucknell, Barry, 207
builders, 6, 8, 21, 24, 38,
    39, 73, 77, 78, 112,
    119, 126, *126*, 163,
    170, 172, 181, 190,
    191, 202, *203*, 218,
    222
bull's-eye, 104, *105*
Bulova, Joseph, 194
bungalow, *100*, 101
Bungalow Taylor, 40–4
burglar, 19
Burslem, 46
butt hinge, 21, *21*
Byland Abbey, 61

Cadbury, George, 132, 137,
    170–80, *179*
Calgary, 110
California, 44, 170
Camisards, 27

carpet, 46, 58, 79–86, *84*
car-port, 32
Carrier, Willis Haviland, 5,
    100
Carshalton House, 133
caryatids, 20
cat flap, 13
cement, 72–9, *74*, *76*
central heating, *3*, 91–102
Ceylon, 42
chair, 31, 34, 48, 49
Chambers, Sir William, 47
Chance, Robert Lucas, 6, 106
Charlemagne, 40
Chatsworth, 133
Chatworth House, 32
Chedworth, 162, 163
Cheltenham, 20
cherub, 20
child labour, 84, 90
chimney, 86–91, *87*
    rudimentary, 118
    sweeps, *90*
China, 59, 77
Chippendale, 48, 49
cholera, 124
Chorley, 98
Chubb detector lock, 16, *17*
Chubb, 15–20, *20*
Chubb, Jeremiah, *16*, 18
Chubb, John, 15
Cincinnati, 79, 134
Claremont House, 96
clay tiles, 69–72
Cliffe Vale, 132
Clyde, 124
Coade, Eleanor, *3*, 20–7, 23
Coadestone, *25*
Coalbrookdale, 199
Cole, Henry, 51
colonial style, 57
Colorado, 125
colour schemes, 44
column, *33*, 37
concrete, 73, 77, 78, 79, 80,
    115, 129, 162, 182

Conran, Terrence, 102
cornice, 37
corona, 37
cottage, *67*
country cottage, 33, 41, 58,
    65, 66, *67*, 68, *68*, 69,
    71, 84, 98, 103, 127,
    149, 159, 170, 174,
    189, 192, 193, 202,
    209, 212, 221, 222,
    224, 230
Country Home, The, 10
Country Style, 65–8
Cradley, 220
Cragside, 143, *145*
Crane, Walter, 56, 65
'crapper', *123*
Crapper, Thomas, 125
cremation, 160
Crete, 125
crime, 18
Crown, 57
Crystal Palace, 93, 108
cupboards, 31
curtail, 121
cyma reversa, 37
cyma, 37

da Vinci, Leonardo, 35
dado, 35, 37, 40
Dalen, Nils Gustaf, *195*, 195
Daily Mail, 191
Daily Mail Ideal Home
    Exhibition, 137
damp, 73, 79, 172, 205,
    211, 215
Danby, 212
Danes, 122
Davidson, Emily, 157
Davis, Henry, 13
de Caus, Salomon, 40
de Morgan, William, 65
de Saint-Phalle, Niki, 56
Death Watch beetle, 211
Delft, 2, 57, 59
Denmark, 166

dentil, 37
Depression, The, 30, 110, 172
Derbyshire, 47
Design Reform Group, 51
Devon, 40, 79
Devonshire, 189
Devonshire, Duke of, 32
Dickens, Charles, 15, 94, 140
Dilettanti Society, 45
Dockwra, William, 11
dog door, 13
dog gates, 121
do-it-yourself, 40, 202–11, 203, *206*, *208*
  dangers, 209
door, 9–13, *10*, 21, 44, 48, 170
  automatic, 20
  knockers, 9, *10*, 13, *14*
  panel and frame, 11
  panelled, 21
Dordogne, 70
Dorset, 26
Dry, Dr Francis W., 86
Drysdale, Dr, 86
Dublin, 20
Dumbarton, 107
Duplex, 155
Dutch, 71, 192
Dutfield, Harry, 84, *85*

East Anglia, 71, 129
Eastlake, Charles Locke, 1, 4, 9, 51, 64, 189, 204
Edison, Thomas, 8, 79, 96, *147*, 149
Edward VII, King, 122
electric bell, 10–11
electric clock, 194
electric light, *153*
Electrical Association for Women, 156
electricity, 176, 177
electrics, 143–60

encaustic tiles, 61, 62, 63
Enfield, New Hampshire, 31
English Rose fitted kitchens, 186, 188
entrance way, 20
Essex, 71
Estonia, 9, *10*
Estonian, 40

faience, 59
fanlight, 44
fascia, 37
federal style, 44, 48
Feetham, William, 139
Feng Shui, 200–1, *200*
fibreboards, 168
Fiennes, Celia, 111, 133
fillet, 37
finials, 20
fireplace, 3, *3*, 5, 26, 44, 61, 64, 88, 89, 90, 98, 102, 119, 143, 207, 209
fitted bathroom, 191
fitted carpets, *82*
fitted kitchens, 181–9
floorboards, 218
floors:
  carpet, 79
  cloth, 80
  concrete, 77
  earth, 72
  pine, 72
Florida, 101
Fowles, John, 26
France, 52, 159, 71, *71*, 80, 86
Franklin, Benjamin, 91, 134, 213–15, *214*
Frederick, Christine, 182
French, 115
frieze, 35, 37, 40
front steps, 20

Galicia, 40
Garden City Association, 178

Gateshead, 76
General Motors, 184, 185
Gentleman's Magazine, 24, 26
George III, King, 26, 47
George IV, King, 26
Georgian colonial style, 48
Georgian era, 112
Georgian style, 113
Germany, 76, 79, 135, 140, 166, 182
ghosts, 121
Gilpin, Revd William, 66
Glasgow, 123
glass, 103–10, *105*, *106*
  crown, 104
  Normandy, 104
  plate, 109
  sheet, 107
global warming, 169
Gothic arch, 38–9, *39*
Gothic Revival, 113
Gravesend, 72
Great Exhibition, 15, 18, 27, 108, 132, 161
Great Fire, 24, 72
Great Paris Exhibition, 125, 149
Great Philadelphia Exhibition, 127
Greece, 45
Greeks, 45
Greenway, 64
Gropius, Walter, 182
Gully, James, 137, 140
gunpowder, 75

häärber, 40
Halifax, 192
hall, 27, 34
Hampshire, 15
Hanley, 132
Hartley, John, 106
Haslett, Dame Caroline, 5, 154–60
Hebridean, 40, *41*

Index

Henry VIII, King, 15
Henry, Joseph, 11
Herculaneum, 24
Hibberd, James Shirley, 51,
    202, 203, *203*
Hill, Roland, 3, 11–13
Hobbs, Alfred Charles, 19
Holboln, 24
Holland, 71, 113
home decorators, 35
home improvements,
    202–11
home insulation, 166
Homer, Winslow, 65
Homo Vitruvius, 36
house style, 35–40
Houses of Parliament, 51,
    62
Howard, Ebenezer, 178
Hudson River, 72
Humberside, 13
Hutton, William, 1, 2, 217
hydroelectrically powered
    house, 143–60

IKEA, 34, 80, 191
Indiana, 31
inglenook, 119
insulation, 2, 162, *167,
    168, 169,* 170, 180
interior design, 49
Ireland, 75
Irish Georgian Society, 116
Irish, 65, 66
Italy, 45, 59, 86
Itamaraty Palace, 118

jasperware, 46
Jefferson, Thomas, 3, 21,
    48, 89, 91, 125
Jenkins, Joseph, 130
Johns, Revd Edward, 125,
    127
Johnson, Dr, 47
joinery, 34
joists, 72

Jones, Inigo, 40
Jordan, 86

Kauffman, Andrea, 46, *47*
Kedleston Hall, 47
Kelmscott, 55
Kelvinator Kitchen, 185,
    186
Kensington, 64
Kent, 43
Kent, William, 118
Kentucky, 31
keyless locks, 17
keystone, 20
Kidderminster, 81
kilns, 74
Kilvert, Revd Francis, 9, 96,
    97, 122
Kirkaldy, 44
kitchen, 1, 2, 3, 8, 13, 17,
    43, 119, 120, *120,*
    132, 137, 156, 159,
    163, 172, 174, 181–9,
    185, 188, 190, 195,
    199, 202, 205, 209
kitchen clock, 189–94
Klargester, 128–9
Klint, Kaare, 34
Knight, Payne, 66

Lambeth, 22, 24
laminate floors, 209
lamps, 149–54
Lancashire, 98
lavatory, 121–30
    euphemisms, 121
    first, 125
le Corbusier, 115
Lee, Ann, 3, 27–34
Leech, John, 139
letter plate, 13
letterbox, 11, *12,* 13
Lever, W.H., 174
light controls, 160, 161
lightening rods, 211–15
Lincolnshire, 11, 71

lintel, 38
Liverpool, 13, 135, 61, 79
London, 20, 61, *64*
Longfellow, Henry, 15
Longhorn beetle, 211
longhouse, 40
Loudon, J.C., 39, 113, 119,
    58, 80, 84
Lyme Regis, 26
Lyncrusta, 58

maiolica, 59
Majorca, 59
Malaya, 42
Malvern, 139, 140
Manchester, 27, 31
Marly-la-Ville, 215
Maryland, 72
Massachusetts, 88, 89
matching styles, 44
Matlock, 66
Mazamet, *71*
medieval hall, 118
mezuzahs, 212
Michelin Building, *64*
Michigan, 100
Minton, Herbert, 4, 61, *62*
    tiles, 57–65
Minton, Thomas, 61
Mintonware, 61
Miracle Plastics, 160
modillion, 37
Mongolia, 80
Monticello, 21, 48, 89, 125
Montreal, 110
Morris, William, 4, 50–7,
    53, 54, 65, 116
    wallpaper, 50–7, *54*
Morris and Co., 144
Mudéjar, 9
Muthesius, Hermann, 56,
    135, 142, 182

nail, 9, 217–20
nailers, 217–20
nail-makers, 219

Index

Nailsea, 106
Nash, John, 24, 68
Nesfield, W. Eden, 146
Netherlands, 59
New Amsterdam, 72
New England, 31, 217
New Jersey, 79
New York, 31, 55, 96, 100, 125, 134, 161, 165
New York Society of Decorative Art, 49
New York Tile Club, 65
New York's World's Fair, 184
New Zealand, 43, 44, 85, 85, 110, 181
Newcastle, 144, 192
newels, 1, 3, 120
Newton, Sir Isaac, 3, 11, 13
Nissen hut, 190
Nissen, Colonel Peter, 190
noggins, 1, 3
Norfolk, 71, 121, 160
Normandy, 217
Northfleet, 72
Norway, 217
nosings, 120
number thirteen, 200

Ohio, 31, 72
Oldham, James, 21
Osborne House, 62
Outer Hebrides, 5, 87
Oval Office, 44
oval rooms, 46
Oxford, 11, 52

Pall Mall, 26
Palladian style, 45
Palladio, Andrea, 37, 45
pallozas, 40
Pankhurst, Emily, 157
Paris, 90
Parker, James, 75
Parkes, Alexander, 161

parlour, 21, 58, 73, 112, 118, 172, 187, 204, 207
paterna, 59
peg rail, 27–34, 30
Pembroke, Earl of, 80
Pennsylvania, 151, 152
Penny Post, 11–13
Pepys, Samuel, 151
Perkins, Jacob, 97
Persia, 80
Perspex, 166
Peshawar, 41
Philadelphia, 83, 96, 213
photovoltaic cell, 176–7
piano nobile, 119
picture rail, 37
Pilkington, 109–10, *108*
Pilkington, William, *109*
pillars, 20
Pincott, Daniel, 22, 24
pinnacles, 20
plasterwork, 34, 44, 46
plastics, 116–17
Pliny the Elder, 103
Pollio, Marcus Vitruvius 35, 36
polypropylene, 169
polystyrene, 166
polyurethane, 166, *167*
Pompeii, 24
porch, 24, 32–3, *32, 33*
Port Sunlight, 178
porte-cochère, 32
portico, 32, *33*
Portland cement, 6, 72–9, *78*
Portland Limestone, 76
Portsmouth, 15, 16, *16*
Potterton, Thomas, 98
power shower, 139–42
pozzolana, 78
prefab, 190–1, *190, 191*
prefabricated, 42
Price, Uvedale, 66
privy, 8, 124, 125, 126, *126, 127,* 172

Prosser, Richard, 63
Provence, 69
public health, 124, 128, 129
Pugin, Augustus, 39, 51, 62, 79
Putt, Lem, 126
PVC, 166, 170
Pyrenees, 70

Queen Anne revival style, 113

radiators, 162
rag rug, 80
Raynham Hall, 121
recta, 37
Red House, 54, 55
Repton, Humphrey, 67
Reynolds, Sir Joshua, 46
Rhode Island, 96
Richardson, John, 174
Rio de Janiero, 26
risers, 120
rising damp, 172
Rogers, Isaiah, 126–7
Roman cement, 76
Roman tile, 69
Romans, 45
Rome, 35, 36, 77
rondevalles, 40
Roosevelt, President, 91
Rose, Joseph, 46
Rossetti, Dante Gabriel, 43, 54
Rotherhithe, 75
Rotorua, *43*
Royal Academy, the, 46, 66
Royal Society of Arts, The, 19, 83
Rumford, Count, 86–91
Ryedale Folk Museum, 212

safe house, 216
St Helens Crown Glass Company, 108

Index

St Paul's Cathedral, 76
St Petersburg, 40
Salt, Titus, 174
Saltaire, 174
Saltram House, 83
Sanderson, Arthur, 57
sash windows, 105, 111–15, *113*
Scandinavia, 27, 34
Scotland, 44, 45, 158
Scott, George Gilbert, *39*
screws, 218
Seddon, John, 43
self-build, 178
sewerage, 128–9
Shaker, 27–34
Shakespeare, 122
Shanks, 121–30
Shaw, Norman, 146
shellac, 164
shelves, 34
Sherand, Robert, 219
shingles, 70
shower, 137–42, *138, 141*
  dangers, 139
Shropshire, 199
Sienna, 215
Sinclair, Sir John, 89
Skanska, 191
skirting board, 35, 37, 40
sliding sash window, *7*
slot meter, 155
Slovakia, *114*
Smith, Gilbert, *128*
Smithson, Alison and Peter, 137
Soane, Sir John, 24
Society for Preservation of Rural Britain, 44
Society for the Protection of Ancient Buildings, 116
solar panels, *176*
solar power, 170–80
Somerset, 71, 90
South Africa, 110
Soviet Union, *37*

space probe, 166
Spain, 9, 57, 71, 93, 137
Staffordshire, 18, 61, 132
staircase, 40, 115–21, *120*
  spiral, 119
stairs, 115–21
  dog-legged, 121
Stamford, 11
Stoke-on-Trent, 61, 63, 132
stone, artificial, 22, 23
stonework, decorative, 20
Stourbridge, 135
Suffolk, 71
Sunshine Homes, 170–80, *173*
superstitions, 200, 212, 213
Surrey, 66, 96, 133
Swan, Joseph, 146, 147, *147*, 149, 154, 164
Sweden, 166, 181, 191
Swinburne, James, 164
Synge, J.M., 193
Syon House, 26

tapestries, 56
tax, 23, 92
  hearth, 92
  house, 92–3
  wallpaper, 92
  window, 93
Taylor, John, 42
termites, 21
terrace, 172
Texas Homecare, 209
thatch, 41, 71, 87
thermoplastics, 166, 169
Thompson, Benjamin, 87, 88
Thoreau, Henry David, 89
threshold, 28–9, *29*
tile:
  Bridgwater, 71
  hollow 69
  mission 69
  Spanish 69

time and motion, 181
toilet paper, 127, 172
Toronto, 7
total design, 46
treads, 120
triglyph, 37
Tucson, 134
tuile à canal, 69
tuile romaine, 69–72, *70*
Tunbridge Wells, 20, 212
Turkey, 80
Twyford, Thomas. W., 127, 130–7, *131*
ty bach, *126*
typhoid, 122, 124

underfloor heating, 160, 162–3, *162*
uPVC, 113, 116–17, *116, 117*

Valencia, 10, 57
Vancouver, 110
Venice, 213, 215
verandah, 100
Vermeer, Johannes, 59, *60*, 114
Victoria, Queen 15
Victoria and Albert Museum, 39
Virginia, 21, 76, 89
Vitruvius, 45, 78, 118
Voysey, C.F.A., 65

Wakefield, 75
Wales, 103
wallpaper, washable, 58
Walpole, Horace, 39, 47
Walsall, 217, 219
Walthamstow, 52
Walton, Frederick, 58
Warhol, Andy, 56
Warwickshire, 174
Washington, 26, 40
Webb, Philip, 54
Wedgwood, Josiah, 46

Wellington, Duke of, 18, 103
Wells, 90
Welsh dressers, 189
Welsh, 115, 189
West End, 24
Westinghouse, 182
Westminster Bridge, 24, 26
Westminster, 19
Wheeler, Candace, 4, 49, 80, 204
White House, the, 40
White, Stanford, 65
Whitmore Hall, 132

Whittock, Nathaniel, 38
Whitty, Thomas, 79–86
Wilde, Oscar, 50
Willenhall, 18
Wilson, John, 140
Wilson, Stephen, 96
Wilton, 81
Wiltshire, 80, *192*
Winchester, 15
windows, 111, 113, 114
    arch, *38*
    disposable, 116
    horns, 112
    Yorkshire sash, 115

Windsor Castle, 62
Winnipeg, 110
Wolff, Heinz, 216
Wolverhampton, 18, 19
Women's Engineering Society, 159
Woodrow, Taylor, 190
woodworm, 211
Worcestershire, 140, 174
Wren, Christopher, 76
Wright, Samuel, 61

York, Duke of, 26
Yorkshire, 61, 71, 115